TO FATHOM THE GIST

Volume III

The Arousing of Thought

—w—

by Robin Bloor

KARNAK PRESS

KARNAK PRESS

Austin, Texas

To Fathom the Gist

Volume III
The Arousing Of Thought

ISBN 978-0-9966299-3-5

Printed in the United States of America

DEDICATION

To Alfred Richard Orage, sine qua non

"The proper reading of this book requires a kind of reading of which none of us is at present at all capable, for we lack the form of logic necessary. The exact sequence of ideas, even words, is necessary—as they appear in the book.

The preface is to the book what the overture is to an opera. Though frankly I did not and you probably will not understand this at all, yet you cannot afford to miss it.

The entire book is a parable, and a series of parables. The 'sower' etc. in the Bible obviously does not refer to agriculture."

~ Alfred Richard Orage

CONTENTS

ignorance is a blessing, an astrological reference, the grammar of associations.

To Fathom the Gist

Volume III
The Arousing of Thought

1

To Read The Tales

"Whatever you are doing, do it as well as possible."

~*Gurdjieff*

—∭—

I n this chapter we shall explore, or better put, revisit, what it means to read *The Tales*. It is not a small undertaking. There are few other books, probably none, that demand so much effort from the reader. Gurdjieff clearly planned it that way, and expended a good deal of effort—having the book read out, observing the responses of the audience, and then editing it—to ensure that the book could have the impact he intended.

In the "introductory notes" of *The Tales*, Gurdjieff explains how to read the book. Our experience suggests that few people, if any, heed his advice. Even when we do as he suggests, almost all of us need to make additional effort before we can read the book well. The book is difficult to read. In our view, this is simply a side-effect of it being an objective work of art. We do not think Gurdjieff deliberately made it difficult; his need to make it objective was overriding.

The Tales as Objective Art

The following is a transcript of Gurdjieff's words from a meeting of his French group, held in 1943. Gurdjieff said:

> "For example, in Beelzebub, I know, there is everything one must know. It is a very interesting book. Everything is there. All that exists, all that has existed, all that can exist. The beginning, the end, all the secrets of the creation of the world; all is there. But one must understand, and to understand depends on one's individuality. The more man can be instructed in a certain way, the more he can see. Subjectively, everyone is able to understand according to the level he occupies, for it is an objective book, and everyone should understand something in it. One person understands one part, another a thousand times more."

> "Now, find a way to put your attention on understanding all of Beelzebub. This will be your task, and it is a good way to fix a real attention. If you can put real attention on Beelzebub, you can have a real attention in life. You didn't know this secret. In Beelzebub there is everything, I have said it, even how to make an omelette. Among other things, it is explained; and at the same time there isn't a word in Beelzebub about cooking. So, you put your attention on Beelzebub, another attention than that to which you are accustomed, and you will be able to have the same attention in life."

Gurdjieff indicates here that *The Tales* is an objective work of art. It is vitally important to understand this when reading it. In *In Search of The Miraculous*, Ouspensky quotes Gurdjieff as saying:

> "In real art there is nothing accidental. It is mathematics. Everything in it can be calculated, everything can be known beforehand. The artist knows and understands what he wants to convey and his work cannot produce one impression on one man and another impression on another, presuming, of course, people on one level. It will always, and with mathematical certainty, produce one and the same impression.
>
> "At the same time the same work of art will produce different impressions on people of different levels. And people of lower levels will never receive from it what people of higher levels receive. This is real, objective art. Imagine some scientific work—a book on astronomy or chemistry. It is impossible that one person should understand it in one way and another in another way. Everyone who is sufficiently prepared and who is able to read this book will understand what the author means, and precisely as the author means it. An objective work of art is just such a book, except that it affects the emotional and not only the intellectual side of man."
>
> "Do such works of objective art exist at the present day?" I asked. "Of course they exist," answered G. "The great Sphinx in Egypt is such a work of art, as well as some historically known works of architecture, certain statues of gods, and many other things. There are figures of gods and of various mythological beings that can be read like books, only not with the mind but with the emotions, provided they are sufficiently developed.

It will help to ponder the meaning of this. The Work seeks to raise the "level of being" of the practitioner. Gurdjieff suggests that even a person who has never met the Work will get something from *The Tales*, but those whose level of being is higher will be able to understand more.

View *The Tales* as a sacred book, as an objective work of art.

Gurdjieff's writings are sacred writings. In an age and within a culture where little if anything at all is treated as sacred, we need to act exceptionally. We need to accept *The Tales* as scripture at a similar level to other sacred writings.

The Philological and Etymological Meaning of Words

The difficulty of creating an objective book in English may not be immediately apparent. It soon becomes apparent if one investigates the dynamics of the English language. The editors of the *Oxford English Dictionary* estimate that several thousand new entries, subentries or edits in respect of usage are made to English each year.

An excellent example of shifting meaning is provided by the word "sophisticated." The root of this and various related words is the Greek word *sophos*, meaning "wise man," and *sophia* meaning wisdom. The word "sophist" derives from the Greek *sophistes* meaning a master of one's craft or skilled in one's craft. But over time *sophistes* came to mean "one who gives intellectual instruction for pay." It became a term of contempt implying someone who makes use of fallacious arguments.

So to "sophisticate" originally meant "to corrupt, delude by sophistry;" around 1796 the meaning "to deprive of simplicity" emerged. Then "sophisticated" as an adjective saw the meaning swing back in the other direction to mean "appealing to people with worldly knowledge or experience" or (of a machine, system, or technique) "developed to a high degree of complexity."

Other examples of significant meaning changes include: "awful," "inspiring wonder (or fear)," now usually means unpleasant or worse. "Demagogue" originally meant "a popular leader". "Egregious" originally meant "something remarkably good, outstanding."

Now consider the word "survey." When Gurdjieff first wrote *The Tales*, it only had the meaning "act of viewing in detail" (from 1540s). The meaning "systematic collection of data on opinions, etc." is attested from 1927. It would typically take another 10 years (to 1937) for this meaning to be confirmed by the *Oxford English Dictionary*. It is thus a meaning that Gurdjieff may never have encountered while writing *The Tales*, although it is currently the most frequent meaning of that word in popular use.

When they read the title of *Chapter XLIV, Beelzebub's Survey of the Process of the Periodic Reciprocal Destruction of Men, or Beelzebub's Opinion of War,* readers will possibly associate to the wrong meaning of the word, in a way that a reader in the 1930s would not have done.

This example illustrates one of the practical difficulties of writing an objective book. Even if it is word perfect when you wrote it, the meaning of words will have changed to some degree within a decade or so of its completion. And with each year that passes, the situation gets worse.

This was a problem that Gurdjieff had to solve - and he solved it. He wrote the book philologically, according to the meaning of his chosen words established etymologically over centuries.

It is therefore necessary for the reader to read *The Tales* with reference to the etymological meaning of the words. We know from long experience that the reader who does not do will miss a great deal.

Consult the etymological meaning of the words.

The Dictionary Meaning of Words in *The Tales*

The vocabulary required to read *The Tales* is higher than most people possess – even well educated people. You might be equal to it, but it is unlikely. Additionally, our interpretation of the meaning of words is habitual, personally associative and often inaccurate.

The extent to which we know the meaning of words is determined by the effort we have put into knowing their meaning. Quite likely, at some point in our education, we were advised to make extensive use of the dictionary. Few of us did. Ideally, whenever we encounter a new word, in reading or in conversation, we should consult a dictionary, ponder the meaning and try to fix that meaning indelibly in our memory. Even if we are just unsure of the meaning we should do this.

However, what is more common is that you will guess at the meaning. You will assume a meaning that the word may not have and proceed to read, uninterrupted by the effort required to ensure that you know the meaning. You may adopt the same habit with sentences you do not properly understand and paragraphs and even chapters.

When reading *The Tales* you have to sacrifice that habit. You must investigate the meaning of words you are uncertain of and even some you may think you know. And, as we have already noted, you need to pay attention to the philological meaning of words.

Do not skip past any word that you do not understand.

You may find it necessary at times—because you simply cannot find a way to understand the text—to make a note, with the intention of returning to it later. There is no point in being stopped dead in your tracks, but you have to resolve to return to it again.

Research into Historical and Geographical References

Research into the meaning of words is not the only research we need to do. Gurdjieff references many things: people, tribes, places, events and so on, that are real rather than fictitious. We will understand his reference, for example to Ex-Kaiser Wilhelm, only if we know a little about the history of that German monarch. When he references something we are unlikely to be familiar with at all, such as the Amu Darya river, we may need to do more extensive research. We need to complete our education where it is lacking.

Beelzebub speaks of ancient civilizations, including Babylon and Egypt, where there is a partial historical record. He covers Greece and Rome, where the historical record is fairly rich. He covers 20th century Russia, France, Germany, Britain and America, where information abounds, but about which we may be relatively uninformed.

Research all of Gurdjieff's real world references.

These real world references provide context to *The Tales*. He would not have included them if he didn't think them important.

The Meaning Conveyed By Punctuation/Typography

Punctuation and typography (meaning style and appearance) are attributes of a written language. There is English punctuation and typography, French punctuation and typography, German punctuation and typography, and so on. For that reason there are distinct differences between the versions of *The Tales* in different languages. In German, for example, there is a typographical rule that nouns must begin with a capital letter.

On its own, this punctuation difference between languages would force the English and German versions of *The Tales* to be different. In practice, they are different in a variety of ways.

Gurdjieff made extensive use of English language punctuation—far more extensive than most authors would do. Most of us may think we understand punctuation, and for normal reading we probably know all that's required. However, for *The Tales* we need to know more. In particular, because Gurdjieff uses specific punctuation to convey meaning, we need to take note of the following:

Gurdjieff's use of full capitalization

This use of all capitals for some words or groups of words (e.g. LORD SOVEREIGN ENDLESSNESS) indicates something sacred or holy, at or near the highest level. The words are capitalized, but reduced slightly in size, so that the visual impact is not disharmonious. It is LORD rather than LORD.

The only other use of full capitalization in *The Tales* is the advert for the school of Mr Chatterlitz, which uses both large and small caps. It is as follows:

I suddenly saw reflected on the sky, by projectors, an 'American advertisement' with the words:

'School Of Languages By The System
Of Mr. Chatterlitz
13 North 293rd Street'

This may simply be a typographical necessity. However, it is also possible that there is a deeper meaning implied by this capitalization.

Gurdjieff's use of initial capitalization

An example of this is the word "Reason." Gurdjieff uses both "Reason" and "reason." Without the capital R it is often "bob-tailed reason." The capitalized word implies a higher level of reason. This usage conforms with the use of initial capitalization in English. The capitalization is a focus, or an emphasis, or amplification of importance. Thus "Reason" is a greater or superior reason.

Gurdjieff's use of quotes

In addition to the common use of quotes, Gurdjieff makes extensive use of "scare quotes:" quotes that indicate that the word or phrase in quotes is a euphemism, or is used in an ironic sense, or simply has an alternate meaning (for example "blessing"). Gurdjieff is suggesting that the reader think about the meaning of that word in its context and not apply the usual literal meaning.

As Gurdjieff uses scare quotes thousands of times in *The Tales*, one needs to pay attention. It is important to identify why quotes are being used and whether their usage has an impact on meaning.

Gurdjieff's use of concatenation with dashes

Compound words are a feature of the German language. Some have made their way into English, such as "schadenfreude," meaning "malicious joy at the misfortunes of others." "Schadenfreude" joins *schaden* meaning "damage" to *freude* meaning "joy," so literally: "damage-joy."

English uses such concatenation sparingly in words like mainstream, screwdriver and waterfall, while German naturally embraces it. It is useful for creating complex concepts. It is clear from the text of *The Tales* that Gurdjieff wanted to construct meaning in a similar fashion. To achieve it he employed dashes, as in, for example, The Terror-of-the-Situation. The meaning of the concatenated words are considered "as if one word."

Gurdjieff frequently uses concatenations that employ noun adjuncts (nouns used as adjectives). He does this frequently with central concepts such as "being," (being-action, being-associative-mentation, being-capacity, etc.) "essence," (essence-conviction, essence-egoism, essence-questions, etc.) and "objective" (objective-being-Being, objective-essence-satisfaction, objective-merits, etc.). He will sometimes use concatenation that threads together many words such as "like-a-puppy-who-has-fallen-into-a-deep-pond."

With such examples, it is interesting to ponder why he felt it necessary to use concatenation rather than, say, wrapping those words in quotes.

In summary, we can say that there are four distinct ways Gurdjieff exploits English punctuation to convey meaning: full capitalization, initial capitalization, the use of quotes and concatenation using dashes.

When considering meaning, take account of punctuation and typography—specifically: capitalization, quotes and concatenation.

Neologisms and Invented (Allegorical) Names

Despite using every mechanism available to convey meaning, Gurdjieff found it necessary to invent some new words and include them in *The Tales*. This can be bewildering to readers, especially as many of the new words are utterly unfamiliar in their construction and difficult to pronounce. The meanings of these words are obviously important, but difficult to discover (we know this from those we have managed to decode).

Although Gurdjieff usually provides an English explanation of the meaning— he does so for almost every neologism—his neologisms often contain a more precise and revealing meaning than given by his explanations. Some of the keys to *The Tales* are buried in these words.

Note also that Gurdjieff used initial capitalization for almost all his neologisms (indicating importance). There are hundreds of neologisms and only 14 do not have an initial cap. Many of the neologisms are compound words formed from more than one language.

The names of fictional characters in *The Tales* seem to be constructed in the same way as the neologisms. They are, in many instances at least, allegorical names that indicate the nature of the character in some way. The name Sakaki for example means "sack of shit." The name Abdil means "servant of the heart."

The meaning of Gurdjieff's neologisms and his invented names needs to be decoded, no matter how difficult that proves to be.

Meaning by Means of Simile, Metaphor, Allegory and Symbols

A simile is a comparison. For example, Gurdjieff writes: "...everything further in this new venture of mine will now proceed, as is said, 'like a pianola.' " When Gurdjieff chooses a simile it is very apt and may be worth pondering.

A metaphor is a figure of speech in which a word or phrase is applied to an object or action to which it is not literally applicable. For example, from Shakespeare: "Now is the winter of our discontent." "Winter" is a metaphor for "darkest time".

An example from *The Tales* is:

> Both these languages are like the dish which is called in Moscow 'Solianka,' and into which everything goes except you and me, in fact everything you wish, and even the 'after-dinner Cheshma' of Scheherazade.

There is a simile and a metaphor here. 'Solianka' is a Muscovite dish. The 'after-dinner Cheshma' of Scheherazade is a metaphor—but for what?

Just as a metaphor is a word used in a non-literal way, an allegory is a story (or poem or picture) which has both a literal meaning and a non-literal 'hidden' meaning. For example fairy tales like *Sleeping Beauty* are allegories, as are Scheherazade's stories from the *Thousand and One Nights*. The whole of *The Tales* is an allegory, which itself contains allegories, some of which contain inner allegories.

Symbols can be thought of as very apt or precise psychological metaphors. Gurdjieff often used his personal set of symbols in conversation. For example, he used the word "dog" on many occasions. (The meaning of this is discussed later.) He was familiar with New Testament symbolism and he uses it throughout *The Tales* in many situations where the reader is unlikely to notice unless they are sensitive to it.

It will help readers of *The Tales* to read Maurice Nicoll's works: *The Mark* and *The New Man*, both of which discuss the symbolism of *The New Testament*.

The Use of Intentional Inexactitudes

Beelzebub explains the importance of intentional inexactitudes in *Chapter XXX, Art.* He deploys inexactitudes throughout all of his written works. When they are encountered they should immediately spark our attention, but in our reading of *The Tales* we often skim across them, not even noticing that something very odd has been placed onto the page.

We do not stop to ask ourselves: "Why did he write that?" If we are to fathom the gist, we need to ask those questions. In our opinion, the importance of Gurdjieff's many intentional inexactitudes cannot be understated. They can be, and often are, keys that unlock doors. They are "puzzles" in the sense that they cannot mean what they seem to mean, so what do they mean?

We note here that sometimes in *The Tales* there are word choices Gurdjieff made that are distinctly odd. We have to take the view that there is nothing in *The Tales* which is accidental. When we encounter an oddity we need to try to put ourselves in Gurdjieff's position and ask: "Why did he choose that word?"

We need to take note of and ponder intentional inexactitudes and odd word choices.

Using Both Legitimate English Versions of *The Tales*

There are only two legitimate versions of *The Tales*: the original 1950 version and *The 1931 Manuscript,* the initial English version that was published and distributed privately. It was sold, with Gurdjieff's permission, by Orage in 1931, to raise money. The revised version published in 1992 is a bastardization, created, it seems, by translating the French version into English. It was not written by Gurdjieff and contains many errors. It has no value and it will only serve to confuse and mislead.

The 1931 Manuscript is more useful than it might initially appear. In it we see *The Tales* "in construction." It can help us understand some sentences that might otherwise elude us. It can also help us appreciate Gurdjieff's work to improve *The Tales*. It contains material that was later deleted that, in our view, has value. It enriches *The Tales*.

Use *The 1931 Manuscript* to help you to understand *The Tales*.

We use it extensively in this book. Juxtaposing *The 1931 Manuscript* against *The Tales* can make it easier to understand the intended meaning.

The Tales and Work on Oneself

Readers of *The Tales* will in most cases also be working on themselves. This has an impact on one's ability to comprehend aspects of Gurdjieff's writings. *The Tales* is thus a natural and helpful companion to one's personal work. One hand washes the other.

In our view Gurdjieff seeks to provoke two distinct changes in the psyche of the reader.

– He wishes to provide new words to employ in our thinking: our "mentation by words." We have few appropriate words in our language for some of the subjects he covers, so he often uses obscure English words or invented English phrases. At other times he invents whole new words. One such word is "egoplastikoori." It relates to the other change he wishes to provoke.

– Understanding the meaning of the word "egoplastikoori" is important to fathoming the gist. He describes this word as meaning "psychic-picturings" and as determining the mentation of our essence, "mentation by form." We believe that his many tales supply us with "egoplastikoori" that can ultimately change that mentation.

Fathoming the gist is not just an intellectual effort. It is a three-centered effort that walks hand-in-hand with other work on oneself.

Reading *The Tales* is work on oneself.

Pondering

In reading *The Tales* (and in The Work) we need to ask questions and ponder. *The Tales* should raise questions for us.

Use *The Tales* to formulate questions and ponder the answers.

In Summary

In this first chapter we have reviewed all the techniques of which we are aware that can assist in the reading of *The Tales*. In the rest of this book we shall apply them to the first chapter of *The Tales*. The goal is to provide the reader with an example of what can be achieved through the collective effort of a group working in the way we have described. Here is a list of the ten techniques:

1) **View *The Tales* as a sacred book, as an objective work of art.**

2) **Consult the etymological meaning of the words.**

3) Do not skip past any word that you do not understand.

4) Research all of Gurdjieff's real world references.

5) When considering meaning, take account of punctuation and typography—specifically: capitalization, quotes and concatenation.

6) The meaning of Gurdjieff's neologisms and his invented names needs to be decoded, no matter how difficult that proves to be.

7) We need to take note of and ponder intentional inexactitudes and odd word choices.

8) Use *The 1931 Manuscript* to help you to understand *The Tales*.

9) Reading *The Tales* is work on oneself.

10) Use *The Tales* to formulate questions and ponder the answers.

The aim of this series of books is not to reveal as much as possible of what Gurdjieff attempts to convey or teach through *The Tales*, but to put readers in a better position to discover such things for themselves.

Throughout this book we refer to Gurdjieff's First Series of writings as *The Tales*, well aware that this is a nickname chosen for the sake of brevity.

In this book we provide notes on *The Tales*, proceeding from the cover of the book to half-way though the first chapter. The primary focus is on the 1950 edition.

We also include notes that refer to the version of *The Tales* that was privately printed and sold by Orage's New York group in 1931—*The 1931 Manuscript*. We discuss both versions, regarding *The 1931 Manuscript* as a work in progress. We also provide some notes on material that was published by Gurdjieff in the booklet entitled *The Herald of Coming Good*.

A convention used for the layout of the book is, where possible to show the text of *The Tales* and *The 1931 Manuscript* adjacent to each other to aid comparisons of the text. Comments on the text are made in the pages that follow.

Despite the fact that the cover shows the name of a single author, the notes on the text of *The Tales* comprise a collective effort by The Austin Gurdjieff Society and a parallel UK group that is an offshoot of The Bradford Gurdjieff Society. As a consequence, throughout this book, the word "I" is never used to refer to the author, only the first person plural, "we."

Throughout this book, the masculine form of the third person is used (i.e. "he" rather than "she") when referring to "man." This is a style choice; it suggests the active principle, which is present in both sexes.

It is expected that readers of this book will have read the two previous volumes: To Fathom the Gist: Volumes I and II. However, the book allows for the possibility that the reader may not have done so.

Two fonts are used: Garamond and Warnock. Garamond is used for text from Gurdjieff's writings, reflecting the fact that it was the font chosen for *The Tales*. All other text uses Minion Pro.

2

The Cover and the Herald's Tale

A man can be given only what he can use; and he can use only that for which he has sacrificed something.

~ Peter Ouspensky

I n the previous chapter we noted that studying *The Tales* alongside *The 1931 Manuscript* could be fruitful. There is also a little additional material Gurdjieff created about *The Tales* which we think worth examining. We are referring to Gurdjieff's description of *The Tales* in *The Herald of Coming Good*, the booklet he produced and distributed in 1933.

This material, written later than the first complete draft of *The Tales*, includes an early version of the prefatory pages (the pages that are printed prior to the start of the book). As you will see, the only overlap this material has with *The Tales* is its version of the contents, which is slightly different from the two other versions of *The Tales*.

However, we need to proceed in a coherent order, so, before we examine *The Herald of Coming Good*, (hereinafter referred to as *The Herald*) we need to consider the cover (the dust jacket) of the 1950 edition of the book.

The Cover of *The Tales*

On the next page we show a copy of the front face of that dust jacket.

It is possible, and in our view likely, that Gurdjieff himself determined to some degree the design of the dust jacket. One of us had a conversation about this with Paul Beekman Taylor, who was a child at the Prieuré. Taylor considered it possible that Gurdjieff designed that cover, noting that, at one time, Gurdjieff created a scrap book for several of his children and illustrated the cover himself. There are several anecdotal stories about Gurdjieff doing design work, including a reference in *Meetings With Remarkable Men* to drawing a monogram on a shield for a neighbor. So it is quite likely that Gurdjieff sketched out a design for the cover and gave it to someone to complete prior to publication.

The actual design was most likely done by Philip Grushkin, a relatively well known cover designer of that era. If you examine the cover on the page opposite closely, his signature can be found in among the swirls below the book's title. For those who are interested, a Google search of his name will provide further information about him. Let us consider this front page, line by line. The main title is:

ALL and

Everything

Note the typography. "ALL" is fully capitalized. We take capitalization to indicate something holy. It seems likely that it indicates OUR ENDLESSNESS as a unity. In contrast, only the first letter of "Everything" is capitalized. It

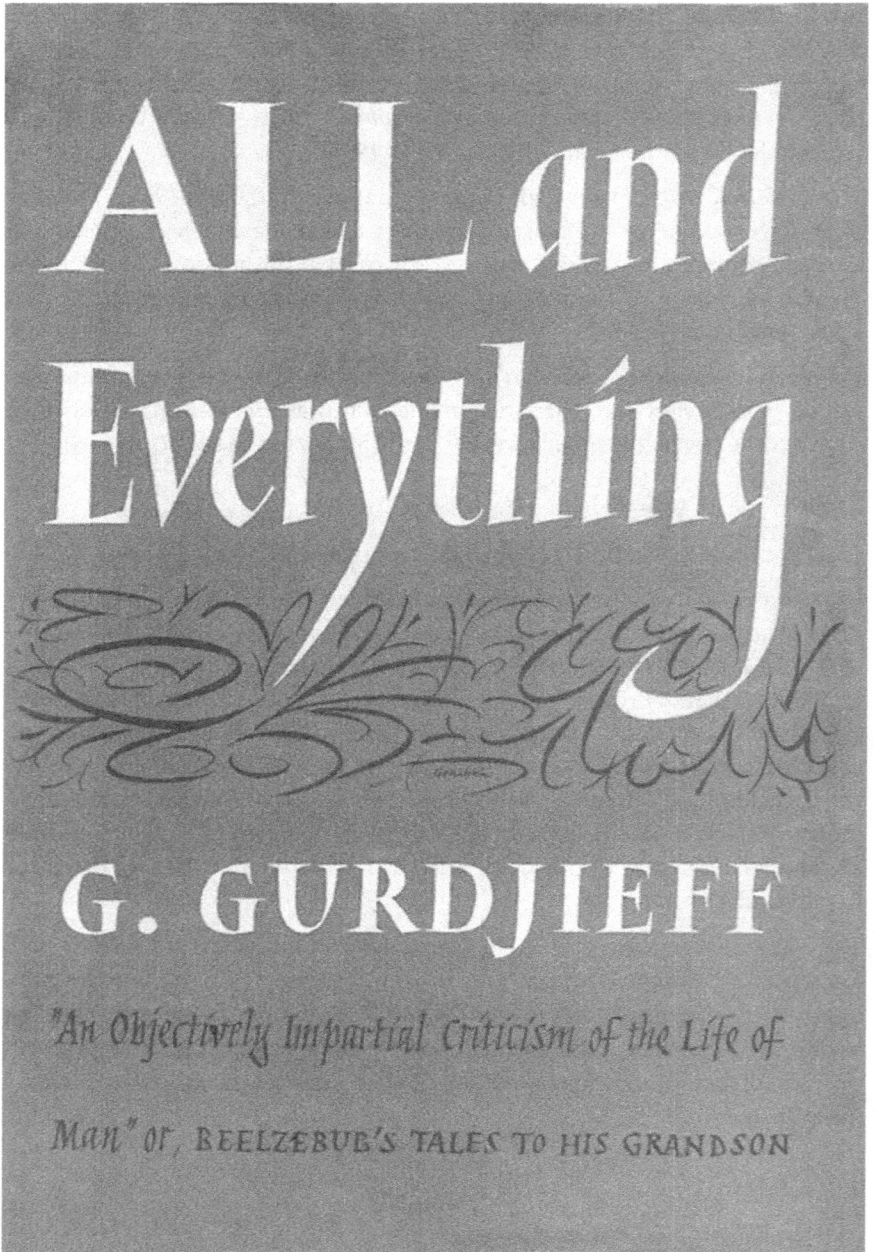

Illustration: The front of the original dust jacket of the first edition

seems likely that "Everything" represents the multiplicity of the Megalocosmos—the fractioning of the everything down to our level and beneath. Of course, this is not the title of the book, but the three series of books, of which this is the first series.

Gurdjieff's Name

Gurdjieff's name is given as G. GURDJIEFF, without the middle initial, and it is fully capitalized. This could be interpreted as normal typographic respect for the author. The font size is smaller than the title of the series, but, unusually, larger than the title(s) of the book itself.

We presume it to be an accidental error that subsequent editions of this book and all other books written by Gurdjieff list the author as G. I. Gurdjieff. This is the only edition of *The Tales* over which Gurdjieff had control of such details, and on the inside pages the name is also listed as G. GURDJIEFF. Gurdjieff had full control over the publication of *The Herald*, and everywhere his name is printed in that booklet it is G. GURDJIEFF.

The spine of the book just shows ALL and Everything and Gurdjieff's name, without mention of the series title.

The Dual Title

Next on the cover is the series title,

"An Objectively Impartial Criticism of the Life of Man" or, BEELZEBUB'S TALES TO HIS GRANDSON.

This is distinctly unusual, for three reasons. First, the font size is smaller than Gurdjieff's name. Second, it is not presented as a subtitle, since it does not follow the title ALL and Everything. And finally, there is not one title, but a dual title.

Dual titles for a book are rare. They were not so when Mary Shelley published *Frankenstein; or, The Modern Prometheus* in 1818. And they still occur occasionally as in: *Dr. Strangelove or: How I learned to stop worrying and love the bomb.* Or the play, *The Goat or Who is Sylvia.* Literary convention designates the first of the two titles to be the real title and the second to be a subtitle. So, on occasion, publishers of Frankenstein have dropped the second part of the title. Nevertheless, the reality is that a dual title means whatever the author intended and thus should probably be left undisturbed.

Gurdjieff chose *"An Objectively Impartial Criticism of the Life of Man"* to be the primary title and *BEELZEBUB'S TALES TO HIS GRANDSON* to be the alternative. The only time he references the book without mentioning both titles is in the book itself, where he mentions just the primary title:

> *"Or again, a being whose love resembled that of a contemporary terrestrial suitor for a rich widow—of course before he has received a single penny from her—would turn just as spiteful as one of those malicious persons who, foaming at the mouth, will hate that poor author who is now writing about you and me, in his work entitled An Objectively Impartial Criticism of the Life of Man.*

The Tales p973

We note here that the primary title is wrapped in quotes and the alternative title is not. Since *"An Objectively Impartial Criticism of the Life of Man"* is not something some individual has said, these are shock quotes, indicating that Gurdjieff wishes us to ponder the meaning of these words.

"An Objectively Impartial Criticism of the Life of Man"

Objectively: The meaning of "objectively" is "in a way uninfluenced by personal feelings or opinions."

Impartial: The meaning of "impartial" is "fair and just."

Criticism: The meaning of "criticism," when it does not refer to a review of a literary or artistic work, is: "an expression of disapproval of someone or something based on perceived faults or mistakes." It has negative overtones. The etymology goes back to the Greek *kritikos* referring to someone who is able to make judgements.

Life of Man: In the juxtaposition of "Life" and "Man," the word "Man" clearly denotes human beings in general, and thus we can take "Life of Man" to denote not just the span of time between birth and death, but also how modern human beings in general live their lives.

So, taken together, we receive the impression that the book will discuss the faults and errors of modern man and will do so without being influenced by any of Gurdjieff's personal feelings or subjective opinions and it will do so in a just manner.

BEELZEBUB'S TALES TO HIS GRANDSON

Tale: A tale is a narrative or story that may be true or otherwise. It can be used in the sense of simply communicating (a statement), or entertaining the listeners (with a narrative), or teaching (as in recounting a fable).

22

Beelzebub: The choice of Beelzebub as the protagonist of the story is partly explained by Gurdjieff in the first chapter, so we will leave it until later in this book to discuss that.

Grandson: Some commentators have suggested that Beelzebub represents Gurdjieff and that his grandchildren are the modern people of the Work who were born too late to ever meet Gurdjieff and hence to whom he can only speak through his writings. This theory implies that Gurdjieff's immediate pupils were his children and their pupils and pupil's pupils are his grandchildren.

Capitalization: Because this title is capitalized, we are inclined to regard it as referring to a sacred collection of tales.

Or

One theory for the existence of two titles for the first series is that this series is, in reality, two books woven together.

The first book is, as the primary title suggests, a withering criticism of many aspects of the life of both historical and modern man. If you were so inclined, you could take note of every criticism that Beelzebub makes of priests, scientists, doctors, kings, emperors, politicians and so on, and you would have an inventory of human failings.

The second book is, as P L Travers called it in her description of the book, published in *The Gurdjieff International Review*, a "great, lumbering flying cathedral." Its central arc is the flight of the Karnak and Beelzebub's recounting of his experiences with "the three-brained beings of planet Earth." It is an allegory, within which there are allegories, within which there are allegories. Included is a full creation myth and many obscurely described scientific ideas and information.

The first book is quite accessible to the reader who dares to persevere. The second book is where "the dog is buried."

* * *

Gurdjieff's Introduction to *The Tales*

From here onwards, contiguous excerpted text will be shown on left side pages, or where necessary side-by-side, to enable comparisons between the two versions of *The Tales*. The commentary and notes we provide will tend to occupy this side of the page, although on occasion it may flow around the excerpted text boxes onto left side pages. We start with the pages from *The*

The Herald

From all that I have already said about this, I shall repeat, in this given case, only in brief the main reasons which obliged me at that time to begin writing and even to become finally a " standard writer."

Some months after the above-mentioned motor-accident, when I myself, and all the people near me, became certain that I would live, and when all the former crystallized functions and the established tempo of the intensive activity of my spirit began, day by day, to be more and more re-established, while my physical body still remained quite helpless, thus producing disharmony between the state of my body and my spirit, and making me very often experience moral sufferings, I decided to find for myself an occupation which would give my thoughts another direction and thus diminish these moral sufferings.

One night, while still in bed and suffering from the insomnia which was habitual to me at that time, stirred by association, and remembering a thought concerning a plan which, during the last two or three months, had always perturbed me and finally even obsessed me—and which should have been realized at the time when I drew up the general scheme of means for attaining the aforesaid fundamental aim of all my life, which included the intention to spread the essence of my ideas also by means of literature, and which failed on account of the untrustworthiness and vicious idleness of those people whom I had specially prepared during many years for that specific purpose—it suddenly occurred to me that there was no reason why I should not take advantage of the present situation and should not begin to dictate myself the material for the realization of this aim.

Consequently, continuing to ponder, I finally decided that I would do so.

The following evening I asked one of the people near me to take a pencil and notebook and to write down exactly all that I would dictate.

At first, intending to spread the different aspects of my ideas in the form of short scenarios suitable for theatre or cinema, I dictated at the beginning such scenarios, and began to "bake" every other day a fresh and completed scenario. I shall mention only four of the numerous scenarios dictated by me :

The Cocainists

The Chiromancy of the Stock-Exchange

The Unconscious Murder

The Three Brothers

Herald, where Gurdjieff explains his motivation for writing *The Tales*, which are shown opposite.

An Inner State

The sentence fragment below, is a good example of Gurdjieff providing a (we presume) precise description of his inner state.

> *...and when all the former crystallized functions and the established tempo of the intensive activity of my spirit began, day by day, to be more and more re-established, while my physical body still remained quite helpless, thus producing disharmony between the state of my body and my spirit, and making me very often experience moral sufferings, I decided to find for myself an occupation which would give my thoughts another direction and thus diminish these moral sufferings.*

These gems are easy to breeze past, but are better pondered. The one above is notable because Gurdjieff may be providing a three center description of his state.

Question: What are moral sufferings? How does it feel to experience moral sufferings?

Previous Writing Projects?

The following sentence fragment is curious:

> *...the aforesaid fundamental aim of all my life, which included the intention to spread the essence of my ideas also by means of literature, and which failed on account of the untrustworthiness and vicious idleness of those people whom I had specially prepared during many years for that specific purpose...*

If Gurdjieff did indeed, as the text suggests, embark upon some literature project prior to *The Tales*, we have not encountered any record of it.

Neither, aside from this mention in *The Herald*, have we encountered any evidence of the short scenarios he mentions: *The Cocainists*, *The Chiromancy of the Stock-Exchange*, *The Unconscious Murder* and *The Three Brothers*.

In a footnote to *The Tales* (both versions), there is a reference to a book Gurdjieff states his intention to write, called *The Opiumists*. This is the only other written work of his own that Gurdjieff refers to in any of his writings.

—————— *The Herald* ——————

To give at least an approximate idea of the character of these, so to speak, small "literary compositions" which I dictated then, and which will also become known to the public in due time, and the subjects of which were often formed in my mind under the influence of this or that impression on my organs of perception, which at that period were particularly sensitive, I find it sufficient to speak here about an event which inspired me to express certain thoughts derived from my ideas, in the last of the above-mentioned scenarios, entitled "The Three Brothers."

Some weeks after I had begun my dictation, when this new occupation not only contributed to put an end to the concentration of my thoughts on my desperate state and on the situation from which I saw no way out, but soon took on the character of a "not-to-be-trifled-with" enthusiasm, and, in the end, resulted in the re-establishment of the disharmonized functions of my physical body which proceeded in an accelerated tempo, I decided, although I could not yet move alone, in order to rest from active thinking and to obtain generally a change of impressions, to go to Paris by car, accompanied by some of the people close to me.

Sitting one evening, during one of these visits, in the Cafe de la Paix, famous then for foreigners, with some friends, we were discussing all kinds of questions.

Among other things was mentioned a film, popular at that time, called "Two Brothers," and one of my companions suggested that we should go and see this famous film, which was being shown at a cinema specially arranged for it.

We all decided to go and, as the cinema was quite near, I walked to it, although with great difficulty. There was an incredible crush in the cinema, the tickets were difficult to get, but one of my companions managed to get hold of some, paying, apparently, an "astronomical" sum.

I do not consider it necessary to repeat here the contents of that nonsense, which was the "pick" of the season. but I must say that sitting in that room overcrowded with people who, on account of bad ventilation were obliged to breathe bad air, I, unable to get out, was compelled willy-nilly to look at the film, and to look intensely, for the focus of my sight was not yet re-established, and I had to fix the various objects sometimes with one eye and sometimes with the other, and the whole time I "felt revolted by such senseless fashionable bluff," the popularity of which was due entirely to the herd-instinct, especially prevalent among people today.

Below are the references to *The Opiumists* in the footnote at the end of *Chapter XLI, The Bokharian Dervish Hadji-Asvatz-Troov.*

> *[Note: If anyone is very interested in the ideas presented in this chapter, I advise him to read, without fail, my proposed book entitled The Opiumists, if, of course, for the writing of this book there will be sufficient French armagnac and Khaizarian bastourma.*
>
> *THE AUTHOR]*

The Tales p917

> * *If anyone is greatly interested in the ideas mentioned in this chapter, then I advise him to read without fail, my book entitled 'The Opiumists,' that is, of course, if I ever write this book, as I intend. Author.*

The 1931 Manuscript p696

More About Inner State

Another comment on state:

> *...when this new occupation not only contributed to put an end to the concentration of my thoughts on my desperate state and on the situation from which I saw no way out, but soon took on the character of a "not-to-be-trifled-with" enthusiasm, and, in the end, resulted in the re-establishment of the disharmonised functions of my physical body which proceeded in an accelerated tempo,...*

The Film

Gurdjieff is referring to a real film, called *The Two Brothers*, also called *Die Brüder Schellenberg* (*The Brothers Schellenberg*), based on a novel by Bernhard Kellermann. It was German, directed by an Austrian, Karl Grune with Conrad Veidt playing both brothers. The text suggests (expensive tickets, incredible crush) that Gurdjieff may have attended the premiere. As the film was made in 1925, that would be consistent with it being some time after Gurdjieff's car accident in 1924.

The Three Brothers and Beelzebub's Tales

Gurdjieff's conception of The Three Brothers is clearly allegorical. Aside from the first chapter of *The Tales, The Arousing of Thought*, this is the only text of

The Herald

At the close of this, what I should call, "general hypnotic-process," in order to fix firmly some formerly suggested ideas, I, "hobbling" and supported by my companions, returned to the Cafe de la Paix, which later became my Paris "office,"and regaining gradually my calm, began to form in my mind the outline of the scenario which I have called "The Three-Brothers."

In this scenario three brothers act instead of two, and all their manifestations and inter-relations are compared by me to the manifestations and inter-relations of the three separate, independently formed and relatively educated parts of man's general entirety, representing, in fact, firstly, the physical, secondly, the astral, and thirdly, the mental body of man; and, in the dialogues of the three characters, in the form of a discussion, that is, affirming and denying, I introduced certain ideas which have come down to us from ancient times, when the science of medicine was very highly developed, ideas of what is useful or harmful, satisfactory or unsatisfactory for one or other of the characters of the scenario in the process of transforming of this or that substance.

During the first two or three months, obliged to dictate owing to my weakness, I set forth, without a definite system, ideas taken separately from the general totality—fragments, in the form of small scenarios, representing various external episodes in the lives of different people.

But later on, when my physical strength was more or less re-established, I began to write myself; and then, during the reading aloud of one of these scenarios of mine, the subject of which was a legend I had heard in childhood about the appearance of the first human beings on Earth and of which I had made Beelzebub, as a likely witness of this appearance, the principal hero, I perceived in that scenario a very rich source from which might be extracted numberless corresponding points of departure for an easy comprehension of explanations of various facets of my ideas, and decided, therefore, to cease writing small scenarios and to write a master-work, taking this scenario as the foundation for all my further writings.

From that time on, exploiting to the full this source for a logical development of one or another of the questions, which, in their totality, might provide a clear understanding of the essence of my ideas, I began to expound and elaborate all the material beforehand selected for publication, following this time a definite system.

which we are aware where Gurdjieff describes his writing process - and he provides just a few paragraphs.

The Three Brothers is thus an allegory for the interactions of the three centers of man. And, in formulating a dialogue between them, Gurdjieff is able to introduce other ideas. Proceeding to formulate small scenarios, Gurdjieff bases one on

> ...a legend I had heard in childhood about the appearance of the first human beings on Earth and of which I had made Beelzebub, as a likely witness of this appearance, the principal hero, I perceived in that scenario a very rich source from which might be extracted numberless corresponding points of departure for an easy comprehension of explanations of various facets of my ideas..

Scenario: This word now has two meanings. The primary meaning is the "sketch of the plot of a play." Its other meaning, "an imagined situation," was first attested in 1960, years after Gurdjieff's time.

The Final Form

In excerpt shown (next page) Gurdjieff writes:

> ...only last year did I finally adopt the text and the final form in which my writings will be published.

Since *The Herald* was published in 1933 this implies that work was completed on the text of *The Tales* in 1932, not long after *The 1931 Manuscript* was being sold by Orage to his pupils. That there were significant changes in the text of *The Tales* after *The 1931 Manuscript* is clear from the chapter names shown in *The Herald*.

Inexactitude

Gurdjieff states incorrectly that work on the book was finished. Of course it may be that when he wrote that it was his intention to do no more work on the text. It may even be the case that the publishers held a "complete manuscript" and were ready to print, but that the order to do so never came - but that seems unlikely.

It is also possible that he was intentionally misdirecting the reader. There is other text that we need to consider in order to have a full picture of this, and this text is to be found in the next few pages of *The Tales*.

The Herald

Since then, during all those years, until today, I occupied myself exclusively with writing, and often, on account of new plans which suggested themselves in the course of my meditations, I changed the text, as well as the outward form, of what was already written, and only last year did I finally adopt the text and the final form in which my writings will be published.

To give the reader immediately, in this booklet, an idea of this finally selected form of all my writings, and at the same time not to strain again my poor brain, which is already tired out, I shall simply give here the first six title-pages of the writings of my first book, which is completely finished and given to the printer.

3

The Title Pages

"Philology is a better route to truth than philosophy."

~ Gurdjieff

—⚡—

The Tales

G. GURDJIEFF

All and Everything

Ten Books, in Three Series, of which this is the First Series

———

Original written in Russian and Armenian. Translations into other languages have been made under the personal direction of the author, by a group of translators chosen by him and specially trained according to their defined individualities, in conformity with the text to be translated and in relation to the philological particularities of each language.

The title pages set out in *The Herald* and *The Tales* are roughly equivalent, and the text is fairly similar. There are no equivalent pages in *The 1931 Manuscript*, which was sold by Orage on a chapter by chapter basis, without these title pages. In this chapter we discuss both versions of title pages up to but not including the contents pages.

The First Page

What is labelled as "first page" in *The Herald* is two pages in *The Tales*. We have indicated this by inserting a line where the page change occurs. So, as presented in the 1950 edition, the title of the book is "All and Everything" and its "subtitle" is:

Ten Books, in Three Series,
of which this is the First Series

In *The Herald* the subtitle is slightly different and so is the capitalization. We note here that the capitalization in the "ALL and Everything" of the cover never made it onto the title page of the 1950 edition or into *The Herald*.

The Herald

First page

G. GURDJIEFF.

ALL AND EVERYTHING

Ten books
in three series.

The original is written in Russian and Armenian. Translations into other languages have been and are still being made under the personal direction of the author himself by a group of translators specially trained in conformity with their denned individuality, and chosen according to their understanding of the text of what is translated, and the philological peculiarities of each language.

PARIS.
1933.

The Philological Declaration

In the 1950 edition, the second title page, is the copyright page. It is here that we find what we call "the philological declaration" hidden under the copyright notice which is as follows:

We use the word "hidden" deliberately. If this is important text, as Gurdjieff suggested by including it in *The Herald*, then it's a surprise that Gurdjieff does not call attention to it in the 1950 edition, but instead secretes it on a left hand copyright page that few readers even glance at.

It has the hallmarks of one of Gurdjieff's "deceptions." Only the attentive reader will notice it and read it. And even one who does is unlikely to pay much attention to it, since on the surface all it seems to say is "I wrote it in

33

Russian and Armenian, and I personally supervised the translation to ensure it was done well."

Differences

If we examine both versions, we notice *The Herald* version is written in the present tense, indicating that work on the translations is on-going. In the 1950 edition, it is in the past tense, indicating that the activity is over. Clearly, in the sense that Gurdjieff would be able to supervise the activity, it was indeed over by 1950, and the only two versions known to be complete were the English and German versions.

The meaning is distinctly different in one other respect. In *The Herald* he writes:

> *...specially trained in conformity with their denned individuality, and chosen according to their understanding of the text of what is translated, and the philological peculiarities of each language.*

In *The Tales*, he writes:

> *...specially trained according to their defined individualities, in conformity with the text to be translated and in relation to the philological particularities of each language.*

In *The Herald* he implies that the translators have some understanding of the text, but in the 1950 edition, he doesn't.

He swaps the word "peculiarity"—meaning "an odd or unusual feature"—for "particularity"—meaning "the quality of being individual." This appears to be a better word choice.

> **denned:** This is an unusual word choice as it is a rarely used word. It is derived from the verb "den" meaning "the action of wild animals living in or retreating into a den." It is used here metaphorically.

> **defined individualities:** This word choice for the 1950 edition, implies that Gurdjieff defined their individualities for the sake of training them for the work of translation.

The editing change from the word "denned" to the word "defined" appears to be an improvement.

Philology and Meaning

> **philology:** The dictionary defines this word as "the branch of knowledge that deals with the structure, historical development, and relationships of

a language or languages." This is a somewhat unsatisfactory definition in respect of "Gurdjieff's philology," since he had little respect for academic philologists. The etymology of "philology" is from the Greek *philologia* meaning "love of discussion, learning, and literature, or studiousness." This itself derives from *philo*, "loving" and *logos* "word, speech."

Modern philology embraces linguistics (the scientific study of language and its structure). This is a 20th century addition to philology, of which Gurdjieff might disapprove. Philology can also be defined as "the study of literary texts, as well as oral and written records, the establishment of their authenticity and their original form, and the determination of their meaning."

Anecdotally Gurdjieff showed a strong interest in etymology, which is an indispensable part of philology in determining meaning. For example, if you know that a word only acquired a specific meaning in the 20th century and you encounter it in a 19th century text, you know to discard the 20th century meaning.

With *The Tales* we repeatedly encounter the need to explore the etymology of a word. In some contexts it is crucial. One example of this is: "The Law of Catching Up." You will never determine its meaning if you do not examine its etymology to discover that "Catching Up" can mean "holding on high." Its modern use is from sport and that meaning is now completely dominant.

In Summary

It appears that the philological declaration is simply a declaration that the book (which was originally written in Russian and Armenian) was translated with special attention to philology. Consequently we need to pay special attention to philology when we read it.

* * *

The Tales

FIRST SERIES: *Three books under the title of "An Objectively Impartial Criticism of the Life of Man," or, "Beelzebub's Tales to His Grandson."*

SECOND SERIES: *Three books under the common title of "Meetings with Remarkable Men."*

THIRD SERIES: *Four books under the common title of "Life is Real Only Then, When 'I Am.'"*

The Third Title Page

In the 1950 edition this is the top part of the third title page. In *The Herald* it has a page to itself.

Differences

Aside from typography, the only significant difference is the title of the third series, which was changed by inserting the word "Then" followed by a comma. This editing change does not appear to alter the meaning of the title significantly.

Inexactitude

There is a glaring anomaly here that is almost impossible to overlook. The *Second Series*, as published, is not divided into three books and there is no division indicated in the text of *Meetings with Remarkable Men* that could lead one to think of it as three books. With *Life is Real Only Then, When 'I Am'* it seems even less likely that it was intended to be four books.

The Herald

Third page

FIRST SERIES

In three books under the common title of

"AN OBJECTIVELY-IMPARTIAL CRITICISM OF THE LIFE OF MAN"

or

"BEELZEBUB'S TALES TO HIS GRANDSON".

SECOND SERIES

In three books under the common title of

"MEETINGS WITH REMARKABLE MEN"

THIRD SERIES

In four books under the common title of

"LIFE IS REAL ONLY WHEN 'I AM' ".

There is a slight anomaly in the description of the three series in the 1950 edition but not in *The Herald*. The *First Series* is described as "under the title of" whereas the other series are described as "under the common title of." This may simply be an editing adjustment. Since the *First Series* has a dual title, the description of that title as a "common title" (common meaning "shared by") may have seemed slightly wrong. However there may be some other reason. The idea of applying the term "common title" to two series that appear not to be series at all is distinctly odd.

So, what are the other books under these common titles?

Gurdjieff announces the titles of three chapters, that he claims will be included in the *Third Series*, at three different points in *Meetings with Remarkable Men*, but these chapters are not to be found in *Life Is Real Only Then, When 'I Am'*. The titles are:

- The physical body of man, its needs according to law, and possibilities of manifestation. (Meetings—Ekim Bey, p191)

- The astral body of man, its needs and possibilities of manifestation according to law. (Meetings—Piotr Karpenko, p223)
- The divine body of man, and its needs and possible manifestations according to law. (Meetings—Professor Skridlov p243)

These last three chapters of the book may constitute Book 2 of *Meetings*. We have been shown evidence of a manuscript of *Meetings* where a page that simply says "Book 2" is included just prior to *Chapter 7, Ekim Bey.*

The book *Gurdjieff And The Women Of The Rope*, p58, as its subtitle indicates, comprises *Notes of Meetings in Paris and New York 1935—1939 and 1948— 1949*. In the book an entry for Thursday June 18 1936 on page 58 records the following:

> *Last night Gurdjieff to Alice that the three portraits in his "gallery"— Karpenko, Dr. Ekim Bey and Skridlov, from which three full books will flow, represent the astral body of man.*

It seems from Gurdjieff's comment that the three chapters on the physical body of man, the astral body of man and the divine body of man, promised in those three chapters of *Meetings,* may have been intended as three books of the *Third Series*. If so, then the above quote indicates that those three books had not been completed in June 1936. It also suggests that those three books are the missing three books from the *Third Series*. We have no idea whether these three books were finished and if they will, at some time, emerge into the light of day.

The Prince Nijeradze Chapter

Prince Nijeradze was mentioned as one of the Seekers of Truth (or Community of Truth Seekers) in only one place in *Meetings*, in the *Ekim Bey* chapter on page 191. This is shown below.

> *Instead of going, as previously mapped out, in the direction of the Persian Gulf, we went west towards Bagdad, since two of our company, Karpenko and Prince Nijeradze, had fallen sick with fever and were becoming worse from day to day.*
>
> *We reached Bagdad, and after staying there about a month we separated and went off in different directions. Prince Lubovedsky, Yelov and Ekim Bey left for Constantinople; Karpenko, Nijeradze and Pogossian decided to follow the Euphrates upstream as far as its source, then to go over the mountains and cross the Russian frontier.*

There have been suggestions that Prince Nijeradze is Joseph Stalin (born Joseph Dzhugashvili). James Webb, in his book *The Harmonious Circle*, claims that Stalin lodged with the Gurdjieff family somewhere between 1894 and 1899, while at the Tiflis Theological Seminary. There are suggestions that Gurdjieff and Stalin attended the seminary together. Neither of these assertions, if true, provide any reason to think that Prince Nijeradze is Joseph Stalin.

And while Gurdjieff may have encountered Stalin at some point in his life, the timelines of the two men make it seem unlikely. There's no space in Stalin's historical timeline for any of the activities Gurdjieff describes in *Meetings*. He was occupied with Marxist political activities in Tiflis while at the seminary and thereafter.

Gurdjieff's timeline for 1894 reads as follows:

Persia

In January, the Persian expedition begins (Meetings, p183). There are 23 people in the company. Prof. Skridlov is among them (p183). Dr. Sari-Ogli (p184), and Prince Nijeradze (p183), and Karpenko are also there. G.'s meeting with Dr. Sari-Ogli for the first time in this trip is "five years" (p170) before the Gobi desert expedition of 1898 (p165). Having passed through Tabriz, they meet a Persian dervish who turns G.'s "outlook on life completely upside down" (p183).

G. had been following the (Hatha) Yogi teachings of mysticism until then (p185). Having been questioned by the dervish, G. realizes the hitherto one-sidedness of his approach to mysticism (p186) and begins to see the value of a synthetic approach to world mysticism. G. realizes that mystical teachings, if followed without care and proper guidance, could actually harm the person (p189—190). Ekim Bey, to whom G. refers as someone very similar to himself (p177), being fascinated with the dervish (p191), asks him many questions about the "physical body" of man (p191), information that G. decades later promises to incorporate in the Third Series of his writings (but never does).

After a week of this meeting, the company goes to Baghdad, where Prince Nijeradze and Karpenko recuperate from sickness (p191), a month after which, the camp divides. Prince Lubovedsky, Yelov, and Ekim Bey head for Constantinople (p191), while Karpenko, Nijeradze and Pogossian follow the Euphrates upstreams. G. and Dr. Sari-Ogli, with the rest (including Prof. Skridlov?), go toward Khorassan (p191).

39

The extract comes from an authoritative document available on the Internet at *https://link.springer.com/content/pdf/bbm%3A978-0-230-10202-6%2F1.pdf.*

This timeline is deduced from *Meetings With Remarkable Men* and thus may not be accurate. Nevertheless, it gives no indication of Gurdjieff being in Tiflis at any time between 1894 and 1899. So while Gurdjieff and Stalin may well have attended the same seminary, it was probably at different times. We should note, however, that Gurdjieff's actual birth date is uncertain. If taken to be 1872, as given on the back cover of *The Tales,* then Stalin and Gurdjieff would not have been at the seminary together. However Gurdjieff may not have told the truth about his birth year (see later).

Nevertheless, it is almost certainly a coincidence that on March 25 1908, Stalin was arrested while using a false passport in the name of Prince Gaioz Nizharadze. This event is the only evidence we have been able to discover that links Stalin to Prince Nijeradze

According to Wikipedia, Nizharadze (Nijeradze) is the name of a formerly noble Georgian family, stretching back to the late 13th century.

> *A family legend of the Nizharadze, written down in the genealogical work by Prince Ioann of Georgia early in the 19th century, traces the family's origin to the Persian Nizhad who settled down in Imereti, his descendants being named Nizharadze, "the son of Nizhad", after him.*

In the book *Gurdjieff And The Women Of The Rope,* p83, we find the following entry:

> *Friday, July 31 [Katie's Notes]*
>
> *Goaded by the others and by my own curiosity as well, I asked him for the only "portrait" we have not read—Prince Nijeradze, mentioned in the Ekim Bey chapter as one of the portraits in this sequence. In his room he tells me it is not here. At table he tells the others:*
>
> *GURDJIEFF: Do you know what she asked me? She ask for chapter Nijeradze and she not even have checkbook, not even possibility of checkbook. [To me:] You know, for reading this chapter, necessary many zeros. You are too young, too poor. This is a big thing for translation of this chapter alone I spend more money than for all others together—so important it is, I wish it be exact. Already it is translated into twenty-eight languages, each translation I verify word by word. If you wish know, there is even copy on your continent America, one in Persia, and one in Germany. None in your England Mees Gordon, and so far none in France. Maybe will be in French since I remain here, will*

see, later. And for such thing she ask and she cannot even write be-gind on check.

Gurdjieff's mention of the chapter on Prince Nijeradze is enigmatic. It seems to suggest that it exists.

If it does then perhaps—this is pure speculation—the third book of the *Second Series* begins with the chapter on Prince Nijeradze and concludes with *The Material Question*.

In Summary

Following is a list of written works Gurdjieff hinted at but which have not been published, and may or may not exist.

1) The Cocainists (scenario listed in *The Herald*)
2) The Chiromancy of the Stock-Exchange (scenario listed in *The Herald*)
3) The Unconscious Murder (scenario listed in *The Herald*)
4) The Three Brothers (scenario listed in *The Herald*)
5) The Opiumists (proposed book listed in *The Tales*)
6) Prince Nijeradze (unpublished chapter of *Meetings*)
7) The physical body of man, its needs according to law, and possibilities of manifestation (unpublished *Third Series* chapter or book).
8) The astral body of man, its needs and possibilities of manifestation according to law (unpublished *Third Series* chapter or book).
9) The divine body of man, and its needs and possible manifestations according to law (unpublished *Third Series* chapter or book).

***

The Tales

All written according to entirely new principles of logical reasoning and strictly directed towards the solution of the following three cardinal problems:

FIRST SERIES: To destroy, mercilessly, without any compromises whatsoever, in the mentation and feelings of the reader, the beliefs and views, by centuries rooted in him, about everything existing in the world.

SECOND SERIES: To acquaint the reader with the material required for a new creation and to prove the soundness and good quality of it.

THIRD SERIES: To assist the arising, in the mentation and in the feelings of the reader, of a veritable, non-fantastic representation not of that illusory world which he now perceives, but of the world existing in reality.

Second Part of the Third Title Page

In the 1950 edition this is on the same page as the previous excerpt, whereas in *The Herald* it is on the page preceding the previous excerpt.

Differences

Most of the differences appear to be editing improvements: "written" is preferred to "expounded," "logical reasoning" is preferred to "logical understanding," "destroy" is preferred to "extirpate," "of the reader" is preferred to "of man," "acquaint" is preferred to "furnish," "assist" is preferred to "contribute to," "veritable, non-fantastic" is preferred to "authentic and correct." If you have much acquaintance with the editing process you may be impressed with these improvements.

The other distinction worthy of note is the change from "that illusory one, which, according to the affirmation and proof of the author is perceived by all people," to "that illusory world which he now perceives." This removes any expression of doubt from Gurdjieff's assertion that the reader perceives an illusory world.

The Herald

Second page

Everything is expounded according to new principles of logical understanding with the purpose of solving three cardinal problems.

PROBLEM OF THE FIRST SERIES.

Mercilessly, without any compromise whatsoever, to extirpate from the mentation and feeling of man the previous, century-rooted views and beliefs about everything existing in the world.

PROBLEM OF THE SECOND SERIES.

To furnish the material required for a new creation and to prove its soundness and good quality.

PROBLEM OF THE THIRD SERIES.

To contribute to the arising in the mentation and feeling of man of an authentic and correct representation of the World existing in reality and not that illusory one, which, according to the affirmation and proof of the author is perceived by all people.

Cardinal problems

> **cardinal:** This means "chief, principal or pivotal." Its etymology is curious. It comes from the Latin *cardo* meaning "hinge, pivot, key." The summer solstice was *cardo anni*, the turning point of the year. The pole star is the *cardo* of the sky. There are cardinal sins and cardinal virtues.

Gurdjieff does not specifically state what the problems are. Instead he includes their description in his proposed solution. We can state the problems as follows:

> **Problem:** The beliefs and views, rooted in the reader over centuries, about everything existing in the world, hinder or prevent his evolution.
>
> **Solution:** Destroy them.
>
> **Problem:** The reader requires appropriate material in order to create a new way of being.
>
> **Solution:** Provide the material.
>
> **Problem:** The reader needs to perceive the world as it is.
>
> **Solution:** Help him (his mentation and his feelings).

43

The Tales

Friendly Advice

[Written impromptu by the author on delivering this
book, already prepared for publication, to the printer.]

ACCORDING TO the numerous deductions and conclusions made by me
during experimental elucidations concerning the productivity of the
perception by contemporary people of new impressions from what is heard and
read, and also according to the thought of one of the sayings of popular wisdom
I have just remembered, handed down to our days from very ancient times,
which declares:

"Any prayer may be heard by the Higher Powers and a corresponding answer
obtained only if it is uttered thrice:

Firstly—for the welfare or the peace of the souls of one's parents.

Secondly—for the welfare of one's neighbor.

And only thirdly—for oneself personally."

The Fourth Title Page

The page entitled "Friendly Advice" is placed immediately before the contents
page in the 1950 edition. In *The Herald* it is labeled the Sixth page and occurs
after the contents.

Differences

As to be expected there are editing differences. Most notable is the preference
for "Higher Powers" over "Highest Forces," (note the initial capitalization in
both versions) and "the peace of the souls" rather than the conceptual "peace
of soul."

Inexactitude

As we noted in Chapter 2, Gurdjieff stated in *The Herald* that work on the book
was finished, even though it was not. On this page we have, in square
parentheses, the assertion:

> [Written impromptu by the author on delivering this
> book, already prepared for publication, to the printer.]

The Herald

Sixth Page

A Friendly Counsel written impromptu by the author himself on delivering this book to the printer.

According to many deductions made by me during continuous experiments concerning the perception by contemporary people of new impressions from what is heard or read, as well as according to the sense of one saying of popular wisdom which I have just remembered and which has come down from ancient times to our very day formulated thus:

Every prayer may be heard by the Highest Forces And one might get a corresponding reward only if it is uttered thrice:

First—for the welfare or the peace of soul of one's parents;

Second—for the welfare of one's neighbours;

And only the third time—for one's own welfare.

The use of square parentheses in any text indicates text added by someone other than the author, in order to add clarity to the text. The fact that almost the same set of words appears in the text of *The Herald* indicates that the words were written by the author, and written long before 1950 when the first edition was given to the printer.

One interpretation of this sentence is that Gurdjieff wants us to treat it "as if" this sentence were written by someone else, for the sake of clarity, to explain what follows on the page. There is, however, another possibility which stems from the etymology of "impromptu."

> **impromptu:** In normal usage the word "impromptu" means "without being planned" or "without being rehearsed." However, etymologically, it comes from the Latin *in promptu*, which means "in readiness," implying that the performer of the act was "ready," even if the act itself was not preconceived.

In reading the sentence we get the impression that Gurdjieff, delivering the final draft of the book for publication, suddenly thought: "Hmm, maybe I should add a little advice at the beginning on how to read the book." Concluding it was a good idea he immediately dashed off a few paragraphs and added them at the beginning of the manuscript. This could not have been the case.

So there may be another meaning. An alternative emerges if we consider the meaning of the word "on."

On: It will be a surprise to most readers that the preposition "on" has twelve possible meanings. They are as follows:

1. "in physical contact with"—as in "she was lying on the floor."
2. "forming a part of"—as in "she had a scratch on her arm."
3. "as a member of"—as in "she served on the board."
4. "having something as a target or focus"—as in "she kept her eyes on the prize."
5. "having something as a medium of storage or transmission"—as in "she stored his name on her computer."
6. "in the course of"—as in "she was on her way."
7. "indicating the day or part of a day when an event occurred"—as in "she did it on Thursday morning."
8. "engaged in"—as in "she was on an errand."
9. "regularly taking"—as in "she was on a course of antibiotics."
10. "will be paid for by"—as in "the drinks are on her."
11. "added to"—as in "the sales tax put a few cents on the price."
12. "having as a topic"—as in "the author wrote his advice on delivering the the book to the printer."

We conclude that meaning 12 is the most likely meaning intended for the word "on" in Gurdjieff's comment:

> "Written impromptu by the author on delivering this book, already prepared for publication, to the printer."

The intended meaning would then be that the friendly advice was written in readiness, on the topic of delivering the book to the printer.

What is Heard and Read

Next we encounter the words:

> According to the numerous deductions and conclusions made by me during experimental elucidations concerning the productivity of the

perception by contemporary people of new impressions from what is heard and read...

Here Gurdjieff declares that he is very familiar with people's perceptions of new impressions in respect of listening and reading, and that he has conducted experiments to understand the process. We should have little doubt that this is the case, given the many reports of him having *The Tales* read out and observing the reaction of the audience.

We then read:

...and also according to the thought of one of the sayings of popular wisdom I have just remembered, handed down to our days from very ancient times, which declares:

"Any prayer may be heard by the Higher Powers and a corresponding answer obtained only if it is uttered thrice:

Firstly—for the welfare or the peace of the souls of one's parents.

Secondly—for the welfare of one's neighbor.

And only thirdly—for oneself personally."

Here Gurdjieff implies that there is a correspondence between the thought behind this ancient saying and the reading of *The Tales*, which relates specifically to prayer. He implies that there is a correspondence between the three modes of praying: for the welfare or the peace of the souls of one's parents, for the welfare of one's neighbor and for oneself personally, and the three modes of reading the book, which he is about to describe.

***

The Tales

I find it necessary on the first page of this book, quite ready for publication, to give the following advice:

"Read each of my written expositions thrice:

Firstly—at least as you have already become mechanized to read all your contemporary books and newspapers.

Secondly—as if you were reading aloud to another person.

And only thirdly—try and fathom the gist of my writings."

Only then will you be able to count upon forming your own impartial judgment, proper to yourself alone, on my writings. And only then can my hope be actualized that according to your understanding you will obtain the specific benefit for yourself which I anticipate, and which I wish for you with all my being.

AUTHOR

How To Read *The Tales*

In these few paragraphs Gurdjieff provides his advice on how to read *The Tales* and all his other books. The word "quite" as in "quite ready" can be taken to mean "thoroughly."

Differences

There are one or two editing adjustments worth highlighting. Gurdjieff changes "writings" to "written expositions," emphasizing (if you consult the etymology of "exposition") that they *"put forth, explain or expose."* He prefers "realize" to "actualize." Etymologically they are both rooted in the concept of bringing something into existence, but the meaning of *"actualize"* is less ambiguous.

Gurdjieff preferred the word "anticipate" to "assume." Again this is more precise, but is less insistent than the word "expect."

Finally there are the changes in meaning that come from the adverbial "firstly, secondly and thirdly," in preference to "first time, second time and third time." The implication in *The Herald* is that one should read Gurdjieff's expositions just three times; in *The Tales* he advises that the reader read in three different ways.

The Herald

I consider it necessary on the first page of this first book which is quite ready for publication to give the following advice :

Read each of my writings thrice:

First time—at least as you have already become mechanized to read all the contemporary books and magazines.

Second time—as if you were reading aloud to somebody else; And only the third time—try to grasp the gist of my writings.

Only then you may perhaps get your own impartial Judgment peculiar to yourself about my writings and only then could be realized my hope that you, according to your understanding, would profit for yourself by the benefit which I assume and I wish you with all my being.

Signed AUTHOR.

Firstly

at least as you have already become mechanized to read all your contemporary books and newspapers.

Even diligent readers read mechanically. It is not done mindlessly—clearly information is absorbed—but it is done without a great deal of attention. It is perhaps worth noting here that *The Tales* defeats some people. They are not able to complete a first reading of the book.

Gurdjieff sees a parallel between reading mechanically and praying:

for the welfare or the peace of the souls of one's parents.

It may be easier to understand this if we refer to one of Gurdjieff's comments about one's parents:

All religions, all teachings come from God and speak in the name of God. This does not mean that God actually gave them, but they are connected with one whole and with what we call God.

For example: God said, Love thy parents and thou wilt love me. And indeed, whoever does not love his parents cannot love God. Before we go any further, let us pause and ask ourselves. Did we love our parents, did we love them as they deserved, or was it simply a case of "it loves," and how should we have loved?

Gurdjieff's Early Talks p419

49

The advice is to read "at least as you have already become mechanized to read" in the same way that one might pray "at least mechanically." Many of our mechanisms are bequeathed to us by our parents. We owe them.

Secondly

as if you were reading aloud to another person

On the surface of it, this is an exercise and not an easy one to carry out. We can read the book aloud to another person, or read it aloud when we are alone, but it is, in our opinion, more difficult to read "as if out loud." And, incidentally, to do this we need to understand the typography and Gurdjieff's rhythm as a writer and how to pronounce the neologisms.

Those who are experienced in reading aloud to others will know that, when one does so, one splits one's attention between the act of reading and the act of listening to the words as you utter them. You attempt to consider the listener and you try to be eloquent. This is a distinctly different and, for some, unusual way of reading a book. It is a three centered activity. The thinking center processes the words on the page, the voice (the moving center controls voice) is modulated by the emotional center and yet no sound is made. Control of one's breathing is also involved.

Gurdjieff sees a parallel between reading in this way and praying:

for the welfare of one's neighbor

This may be easier to appreciate if we refer to the following words that appear in *The Tales*:

> *...the commandment inculcated in me in my childhood, enjoining that "the highest aim and sense of human life is the striving to attain the welfare of one's neighbor," and that this is possible exclusively only by the conscious renunciation of one's own.*
>
> *The Tales p1186*

In our view, in order to read out loud effectively, one needs to be a willing and faithful servant to the listeners.

Thirdly

And only thirdly—try and fathom the gist of my writings

First note that Gurdjieff writes: "And only thirdly," advising that there should be no attempt to "try and fathom the gist" in either of the other two modes of reading.

We may also take note of the change between the version in *The Herald* and *The Tales*. In *The Herald* it says: "try to grasp the gist of my writings." This is changed to "try and fathom the gist."

This is surprising. If the intended meaning is "try to fathom the gist" it is simply bad English, which is not at all likely. Even if Gurdjieff were capable of making such an error, he had Alfred Orage and Jane Heap as his editorial assistants (two extremely experienced and talented editors). They would not have allowed such an elementary grammatical error to pass without comment.

> **try:** Consider the etymology of "try." The original meaning of this word is from the Anglo-French *trier* which meant "to examine judiciously or sit in judgement of" and from which comes the English word "trial." It only later acquired the meaning of "to attempt to do."

> **fathom:** The noun "fathom" is a measure of six feet, which approximates to the length of arms stretched out sideways from finger tip to finger tip. The verb "fathom," from Old English, means "to embrace, surround, envelop," giving the sense of "getting your arms around." It later came to mean "to get to the bottom of."

> **gist:** This is of French origin. *Gîte* is French for a "domicile or habitation" and also has the meaning of something "covert." An associated verb from Old French, *gésir* gives *gist en* (third person present indicative), meaning "it consists in" or "lies in." The "gist" thus came to mean "the heart of" or "the essence of."

To "try and fathom the gist" speaks of two efforts, not one. To sit in judgement over and to get to the essence.

Gurdjieff sees a parallel between reading in this way and praying:

> *And only thirdly—for oneself personally.*

One way of thinking of the parallel between this three-part prayer and the reading of *The Tales* is to think of it in terms of body, essence and reason. The second reading is for growth of essence. The third reading is for growth of Reason.

Only Then

Gurdjieff concludes this page with:

> *Only then will you be able to count upon forming your own impartial judgment, proper to yourself alone, on my writings. And only*

then can my hope be actualized that according to your understanding you will obtain the specific benefit for yourself which I anticipate, and which I wish for you with all my being.

These words imply a promise: as far as the reader is concerned, if he reads it in the manner described, he will be able to form his own "impartial judgement" —a rare capacity the reader probably never possessed before reading the book—and Gurdjieff's hope for the reader, the nature of which he does not specifically state, will be actualized.

4

The Contents Pages

"In properly organized groups no faith is required; what is required is simply a little trust and even that only for a little while, for the sooner a man begins to verify all he hears the better it is for him."

~ Gurdjieff

The Tales

Contents

FIRST BOOK

The Herald

Fifth page
Contents of the first series first book.

The 1931 Manuscript
Contents
BOOK ONE

1. Warning. (Instead of a Preface).
2. Introduction: Why Beelzebub Was In Our Solar System.
3. The Reason Of The Delay In The Falling Of The Trans-space Ship "Karnak".
4. The Law of Falling.
5. The System of Archangel Hariton.
6. Perpetual Motion.
7. Being Aware Of Genuine Being-Duty.
8. The Impudent Brat Hassein, Beelzebub's Grandson, Dares To Call Us 'Slugs'.
9. The Cause of the Genesis of the Moon.
10. Why 'Men' are not Men.
11. A Piquant Trait of the Peculiarity of Man's Psyche.
12. The First Growl.
13. Why, in Man's Reason, Fantasy May be Perceived as Reality.

There are three sets of contents pages to consider: the one that was provided with *The 1931 Manuscript* and those from *The Herald* and *The Tales* itself.

We note, incidentally, that the contents list that was circulated with *The 1931 Manuscript* when it was first distributed did not correspond to the chapters that Orage distributed - probably because the chapters were sold one at a time. Most likely that contents list was distributed with the last chapter. Whatever its origin, it is the contents list that was distributed with the typescript version of *The 1931 Manuscript* that was sold and distributed by By The Way Books.

It does not correspond to the one in the version of *The 1931 Manuscript* published by Karnak Press. That contents list was deduced from the actual chapter titles in its publication of *The 1931 Manuscript*. That publication was not a simple reproduction of the chapters that Orage distributed. Three kinds of changes were made. The first were the eradication of obvious spelling errors and typos. The second was to change all Gurdjieff's names and neologisms to correspond with those in *The Tales*, for the sake of readability. (A full record of all changes made to the original manuscript are provided in the book). The third change was to reorder the structure of some of the text. That was also

The 1931 Manuscript

14. The Beginnings of Perspectives Promising Nothing Very Cheerful.
15. The First Descent Of Beelzebub on the Earth.
16. The Relative Understanding of Time.
17. The Arch-Absurd: In The Opinion of Beelzebub, Our Sun, it Appears, Neither Lights nor Heats.
18. The Arch-preposterous.
19. Beelzebub's Tale about His Second Descent on the Planet Earth.
20. The Third Flight of Beelzebub to the Planet Earth.
21. The First Visit of Beelzebub to India.
22. Beelzebub in Thibet for the First Time.
23. The Fourth Personal Sojourn of Beelzebub on the Planet Earth.
24. Beelzebub's Flight to the Planet Earth for the Fifth Time.
25. The Very Saintly Ashiata Shiemash, Sent from Above to the Earth.
26. The Legominism Concerning the Deliberations of the Very Saintly Ashiata Shiemash under the Title of "The Terror of the Situation."
27. The Kind of Organization for Man's Existence Created by the Very Saintly Ashiata Shiemash.

done for readability. Thus the actual contents list from the Karnak Press's publication of *The 1931 Manuscript* is not included here, as it was never a contents list that Gurdjieff or Orage approved.

We cannot be sure whether the contents pages we are shown in *The Herald* definitely came earlier or later than those we show from the Oragean version of *The 1931 Manuscript*. We have organized this chapter as though the version in *The Herald* is more recent, although it is possible that it is not, or that each came from divergent manuscripts that were later united.

Differences Between the Three Contents Lists

We will comment on the differences between the three different contents lists that cannot be counted as simple editing adjustments as we encounter them.

However, this will not be the only focus of this chapter. We will also make some observations about some of the chapters, observations about the major themes of *The Tales* that are brought into focus by the chapter titles and some observations about the structure of *The Tales* as a whole.

Prefaces and Introductions

As is apparent from all three versions of the contents (see previous page), Gurdjieff does not adhere to the typical style and format for a book. The second chapter (*Introduction: Why Beelzebub Was in Our Solar System*) is the actual introduction to the book. It is preceded by the first chapter, which is therefore a preface of some kind.

Preface, Introduction: The advice of *The Chicago Manual of Style* is:

A preface or foreword deals with the genesis, purpose, limitations, and scope of the book and may include acknowledgments of indebtedness; an introduction deals with the subject of the book, supplementing and introducing the text and indicating a point of view to be adopted by the reader. The introduction usually forms a part of the text [and the text numbering system]; the preface does not.

The first chapter of *The Tales* is actually a preface, but a distinctly atypical one. *The Chicago Manual of Style* lists three different types of preface: a foreword, an editor's preface and an author's preface.

A foreword is typically written by someone other than the author or editor, often someone who is eminent and whose kind words may help to validate the worth of the book. An editor's or author's preface (usually one or the other) describes the book's purpose and scope and expresses acknowledgment of assistance from others.

Gurdjieff violates the style guidelines for a preface by making his author's preface the first chapter of the book. *The Chicago Manual of Style* insists that prefaces and forewords are not integral, but are numbered separately, along with other front matter, using lower-case roman numerals: i, ii, iii, iv, etc.

Gurdjieff's preface occupies 50 pages and employs over 15,000 words. It almost qualifies as a book of itself.

The First Chapter and Its Title

According to Wikipedia, Gurdjieff edited or rewrote the first chapter 30 times. Elsewhere we've seen the figure 13 times suggested. Either way, it is clear that many changes were made between the first chapter published in *The 1931 Manuscript* and in *The Tales*. In the former, its title is *WARNING (Instead of a Preface)*, it occupies just 39 pages and uses about 11,600 words.

It does not qualify as a preface or prologue, but might, as Orage suggests, be thought of as an overture.

The preface is to the book what an overture is to the opera. The ideas to be developed are indicated lightly. The expression is not by direct statement but by parable. Compare Swift's Tale of a Tub. The preface is called a Warning.

The text of the first chapter clearly includes elements of a warning to the reader about how difficult or uncomfortable it may be to read the book, so the title *WARNING (Instead of a Preface)* seems appropriate.

Nevertheless Gurdjieff concluded that *The Arousing of Thought* was a better title. There's little in the etymology of "arouse" or "thought" that is startling. The concept of "arousing thought" is unfamiliar. Is our thinking capability normally asleep and hence requires to be woken up? For most of us, this is indeed the case. The title of the first chapter indicates, perhaps, that Gurdjieff intends to shake it from its slumber.

Ships and Falling

Chapters II to VIII make little mention of "men" or the planet Earth. They are "scene-setting" for the rest of the book and they also say a few things about space-ships that are enigmatic.

Gurdjieff does not use the word "spaceship" at all. "Spaceship" is a relatively new word, probably coined by J J Astor, who used the word in novel called *A Journey in Other Worlds*, published in 1894. Gurdjieff uses "space-ship," or "transspace ship," or "inter-solar-system ship," or "transsystem ship," or "intersystem ship." The word "transspace" is Gurdjieff's invention and has not made it into a dictionary (yet).

Only three ships are mentioned, *The Occasion*, which Gurdjieff uses to go to Earth, *The Omnipresent* used by "the sacred members of the third Most Great Commission" and *The Karnak* which is the ship on which Beelzebub tells his tales to Hassein.

> **Karnak:** According to Orage, "Karnak" means "our body as it is put into the grave" in Armenian. Karnak in Egypt is the site of a great complex of temples, covering about 200 acres. Chief among them is the Precinct of Amun-Ra, covering about 61 acres. (Amun Ra literally means "hidden light," Ra being the Sun god). This is the temple to which the name "Karnak" is usually applied. It was known as Ipet-isu to the ancient Egyptians, meaning "the most select of places." In ancient times an annual festival of renewal was held there, towards the end of the agricultural cycle (winter time). The name Karnak is believed to derive from the Arabic *Ka-*

Ranak meaning "fortified village." Carnac in France is believed to be the largest group of megaliths. It has been suggested that Carnac in the Breton language means "field of flesh," although it could also be translated as "burial place" or "cemetery."

Beelzebub's first two visits to Earth are described as a descents. The other four are described as flights to Earth or sojourns on Earth (a sojourn is a temporary stay).

The means by which these ships propel themselves is described in *Chapter V, The System of Archangel Hariton*. However, throughout most of the book the passage from one location to another is referred to as "falling." This "falling," as literally described, seems a little like the action of gravity, but it is clear from the text that Gurdjieff is referring to something else. The logical conclusion for the reader is that Gurdjieff is employing an allegory.

It is clear from Gurdjieff's description of perpetual motion in Chapter VI that this is part of his allegory. So what does the allegory mean?

The Impudent Brat Hassein Dares to Call Men "Slugs"

Gurdjieff appears to be springing an etymological joke on us when he has Beelzebub point out to Hassein that his calling men "slugs" could lead to terrible consequences. Hassein, after all, was simply using "slugs" as a metaphor to describe a being with oily skin. And it was not by any means a "daring" act. Most men would forgive such a harmless error.

> **Hassein:** The etymology of Gurdjieff's invented name "Hassein" is not entirely clear. It is possibly formed from the Turkish adjective *has*, meaning "pure" or "unmixed," and the German noun *sein*, which can mean "essence" or "being." Alternatively the "Has" may simply be the English "has". "Pure essence" seems likely. We can view *The Tales* as Gurdjieff (Beelzebub) speaking directly to us (Hassein, our essence).

Orage suggests that Hassein is magnetic center. He also says "Hassein is that part of you that is open to the suggestion of another part of you, not yet actualized."

The name Hassein is also suggestive of Husain. Husain and Hasan were the grandsons of the Prophet Muhammad and the two sons of Hazrat Fatima, the daughter of the Holy Prophet. It was the martyrdom of Husain in a battle near Kerbala (in Iraq) and the reverence in which his actions in defense of Islam were held that gave birth to the Shia sect of Islam. There is a pilgrimage to Husain's tomb in Kerbala every year. Referred to as the Arba'een Pilgrimage it is the world's largest public gathering, greater than the annual pilgrimages in Mecca. In recent years over 19 million people have attended.

Impudent: late 14c., from Latin *impudentem* (nominative *impudens*) "without shame, shameless," from assimilated form of *in-* "not, opposite of" + *pudens* "ashamed, modest," present-participle adjective from *pudere* "to cause shame".

Brat: c. 1500, "beggar's child" ("... wyle beggar with thy brattis ...), originally slang, from a northern, midlands and western England dialect word for "makeshift or ragged garment;" probably the same word as Old English *bratt* "cloak," which is from a Celtic source (Old Irish *bratt* "cloak, cloth"). The transferred meaning is perhaps from notion of "child's apron." Brattery "nursery" is attested from 1788.

Slug: "shell-less land snail," 1704, originally "lazy person" (early 15c.); related to sluggard.

Arch-absurd and Arch-preposterous

Gurdjieff's use of the prefix "arch" should be startling. It provokes pondering. In two successive chapters he highlights that something is very wrong, abnormal. The etymology of "arch" as a prefix is:

Arch- also archi-: word-forming element meaning "chief, principal; extreme, ultra; early, primitive," from Latinized form of Greek *arkh-*, *arkhi-* "first, chief, primeval," combining form of *arkhos* "a chief, leader, commander," *arkhein* "be first, begin."

That "the Sun neither lights nor heats" begins in *The 1931 Manuscript* as "an opinion" that is edited to become an affirmation in *The Herald* and ends up being an assertion in *The Tales*. The meaning of this assertion is easier to comprehend if it is viewed as allegorical.

Absurd: "plainly illogical," 1550s, from Middle French *absurde* (16c.), from Latin *absurdus* "out of tune, discordant;" figuratively "incongruous, foolish, silly, senseless," from *ab-* "off, away from," here perhaps an intensive prefix, + *surdus* "dull, deaf, mute."

Etymologically, the meaning of "Arch-absurd" can be taken as the "principal stupidity," or if you prefer, the "great out-of-tune." Gurdjieff is emphatic.

The Arch-preposterous chapter describes the scientific experiments of Gornahoor Harhark. In *The Herald*, it had the title *The arch-fantasy*. The question is why does the chapter have that title?

Preposterous: 1540s, from Latin *praeposterus* "absurd, contrary to nature, inverted, perverted, in reverse order," literally "before-behind" (compare topsy-turvy, cart before the horse), from *prae* "before" + *posterus* "subsequent."

Ashiata Shiemash

Ashiata Shiemash could be regarded as the most important character in *The Tales*. Some commentators identify him with Zoroaster (or Zarathustra) who, according to records, inhabited the same geographical area. There is little that remains of the Zoroastrian religion although it was once dominant across ancient Persia. It was not so much destroyed as absorbed into Shia Islam, in the sense that many Zoroastrians adopted the Shia faith when Islam spread to Iraq and Iran. Shia and Sunni Islam are distinctly different in many of their practices.

The etymology of the name "Ashiata Shiemash" is not easy to unravel. Anecdotally, we have heard it suggested that it comes from ancient Sumerian, and means "Rays of the sun." *Ashia* is Farsi for ray. The *ata* may simply indicate a plural as in Latin. The Hebrew word for sun is *Shemesh*. Putting that all together, Ashiata Shiemash may mean "the light of the sun." It has also been suggested that it means "Sun of Asia," (by Richard Hodges).

In *The Tales* there is a clear intentional inexactitude in discussing Ashiata's mission. Ashiata concludes that the ways of Faith (through Saint Lama), Hope (through Saint Mohammed) and Love (through Jesus Christ) had been tried and now would no longer be effective with Man. This, impossibly in terms of the time line of *The Tales*, places Ashiata Shiemash after Mohammed rather than in the time of Babylon.

It is even possible that Ashiata Shiemash should be placed after Gurdjieff. Consider the following, reported anecdotally by a pupil of Louise March:

> *Louise March related something which took place while she was working directly with Gurdjieff translating The First Series into German. They were working on the passage with Ashiata Shiemash. During the reading of the material, Gurdjieff very earnestly engaged with Louise, pressing her for an answer:*
>
> *"You believe? You believe Ashiata Shiemash?"*
>
> *Louise pondered the question for a few moments, taken aback, then answered him by saying, "Yes. I believe he was real."*
>
> *"Not was," replied Gurdjieff sternly. "Will Be!"*

We can add the following from the records of Gurdjieff's Paris meetings:

> *In the beginning, the sexual act was only meant to be used for the purpose of reproducing the species. But little by little, man made it a source of pleasure. It was meant to be a sacred act. Let us hope that if Ashiata Shiemash establishes his order on Earth once more, it will again become a sacred act.*

It is possible then that Gurdjieff was the forerunner for Ashiata Shiemash.

The Herald

The Division into Three Books

A curiosity that emerges in comparing the three sets of Contents is that *The 1931 Manuscript* and *The Herald*, are divided into three books in a different way than *The Tales*. In *The Tales*, the first book ends with *Chapter XXVIII, The Chief Culprit in the Destruction of All the Very Saintly Labors of Ashiata Shiemash*, while the other two end with *Chapter XXX, Art*. The two chapter disparity rolls forward across book two, so *The 1931 Manuscript* and *The Herald* have two extra chapters in the third book.

So why the difference? One possibility is simply that Chapters I to XXVIII occupy 410 pages, Chapters XXIX to XXXIX occupy 400 pages and Chapters XL to XLVII occupy 428 pages. The decision may simply have been based on splitting *The Tales* so that each book was approximately the same length.

The fact that the early manuscripts were divided in a different way argues against there being some significance as to where one book ends and the next begins. Even so, there does seem to be some significance as to where *The Tales* is divided. The first book ends with the chapters about Ashiata Shiemash, the second with *The Holy Planet Purgatory* and the third with *The Inevitable Results of Impartial Mentation* (if one discounts the epilogue).

Three Themes Woven Together

We mentioned in chapter 2 that *The Tales* with its dual title might be regarded as two books woven together, or more precisely, as a book with two interlocking themes. The context of Beelzebub's tales is set up first with an explanation as to why Beelzebub was in our solar system and how the opportunity arose for Beelzebub to start telling Hassein tales.

It is not until Chapter VIII, when Hassein calls men "slugs," that Beelzebub's narrative starts to focus in on the three-brained beings of planet Earth. From then on the narrative is written in such a way that Beelzebub could just as well be addressing the reader as addressing Hassein, with Beelzebub repeatedly describing men as "three brained beings who have taken your fancy," or "your favorites."

At that point in the book, the two distinct themes become woven together. Beelzebub is able, on the one hand, to describe real or allegorical events that happened on Earth, while being "impartially critical" of the three-brained beings he is referring to, and on the other, to describe events such as Beelzebub's trips to Mars and Saturn that have little to do with men directly.

All of Beelzebub's visits to Earth provide opportunities for Gurdjieff to criticize (or praise) the actions of various three-brained beings. His criticism spans a wide range of topics: religion, science, art, wars, politics, history and health. Much of this would, in the context of the story, be details of Beelzebub's time in our solar system that might interest Hassein, but would not contribute a great deal to his Oskiano (education)—although it is likely to contribute to the Oskiano of the reader.

In *Chapter XLVI, Beelzebub Explains to his Grandson the Significance of the Form and Sequence Which He Chose for Expounding the Information Concerning Man*, Beelzebub says:

> *I, being free from any other being-duties whatsoever, voluntarily took upon myself the responsible guidance of your finishing Oskiano for the Being of a responsible being, or, as your favorites would say, 'your education.'*

Hassein is twelve (Karatasian) years old, an age at which in many cultures the onset of adulthood, sometimes referred to as "the age of accountability" occurs. (Full adulthood arrives with "the age of responsibility.") In many Christian denominations, this is the age at which the Sacrament of Confirmation takes place. In Islam, children reaching puberty are required to perform salat and other obligations—this is generally between the age of nine-to-twelve for a girl, and twelve-to-fifteen for a boy. In Judaism the coming of age for a boy (Bar Mitzvah) is at age thirteen and for a girl (Bat Mitzvah) age twelve.

So Beelzebub's tales are addressed to the reader as if he or she were twelve years old. Because the reader is likely to be far older than that, the text can only educate the reader in the sense of providing them material with which to repair their past.

This "education of Hassein" covers many topics of the Work, providing details which, to our knowledge, are either not found in other Work books, or are described here in an unusual way. It includes the law of three, the law of seven, various other cosmic laws, purgatory and even the creation.

As the book progresses, a third arc rises up and becomes increasingly prominent: the redemption of Beelzebub. Beelzebub was exiled to our solar system because of "the errors of his youth" and he must inevitably pay for that. He tells of his visits to Earth, at the behest of angels and archangels, to try to correct "unforeseeingnesses" on the part of various Sacred Individuals. Beelzebub's actions on behalf of these Sacred Individuals earn him his redemption.

The Tales is thus like a fugue in three voices that intertwine and develop until they complete together at the end. Beelzebub is perfected up to the level of the Sacred Podkoolad, Hassein's education is complete and, at Hassein's request, Beelzebub offers his remedy for the redemption of Man:

> "*The sole means now for the saving of the beings of the planet Earth would be to implant again into their presences a new organ, an organ like Kundabuffer, but this time of such properties that every one of these unfortunates during the process of existence should constantly sense and be cognizant of the inevitability of his own death as well as of the death of everyone upon whom his eyes or attention rests.*
>
> "*Only such a sensation and such a cognizance can now destroy the egoism completely crystallized in them that has swallowed up the whole of their Essence and also that tendency to hate others which flows from it—the tendency, namely, which engenders all those mutual relationships existing there, which serve as the chief cause of all their abnormalities unbecoming to three-brained beings and maleficent for them themselves and for the whole of the Universe.*"

Note:

For the remaining chapters of this book, the text of *The Tales* and *The 1931 Manuscript* are shown side-by-side on the page (*The Tales* on the left and *The 1931 Manuscript* on the right) so that the reader can compare the two versions. Where possible, the text is adjusted so that corresponding paragraphs are adjacent to each other. The text discussed in each chapter is shown before the commentary.

5

The 'Do' of the Octave

"Awakening begins when a man realizes that he is going nowhere and does not know where to go."

~ *Gurdjieff*

—∭—

CHAPTER 1

The Arousing of Thought

A MONG other convictions formed in my common presence during my responsible, peculiarly composed life, there is one such also—an indubitable conviction— that always and everywhere on the earth, among people of every degree of development of understanding and of every form of manifestation of the factors which engender in their individuality all kinds of ideals, there is acquired the tendency, when beginning anything new, unfailingly to pronounce aloud or, if not aloud, at least mentally, that definite utterance understandable to every even quite illiterate person, which in different epochs has been formulated variously and in our day is formulated in the following words: "In the name of the Father and of the Son and in the name of the Holy Ghost. Amen."

That is why I now, also, setting forth on this venture quite new for me, namely, authorship, begin by pronouncing this utterance and moreover pronounce it not only aloud, but even very distinctly and with a full, as the ancient Toulousites defined it, "wholly-manifested intonation"— of course with that fullness which can arise in my entirety only from data already formed and thoroughly rooted in me for such a manifestation; data which are in general formed in the nature of man, by the way, during his preparatory age, and later, during his responsible life engender in him the ability for the manifestation of the nature and vivifyingness of such an intonation.

Having thus begun, I can now be quite at ease, and should even, according to the notions of religious morality existing among contemporary people, be beyond all doubt assured that everything further in this new venture of mine will now proceed, as is said, "like a pianola."

In any case I have begun just thus, and as to how the rest will go I can only say meanwhile, as the blind man once expressed it, "we shall see."

First and foremost, I shall place my own hand, moreover the right one, which—although at the moment it is slightly injured owing to the misfortune which recently befell me—is nevertheless really my own, and has never once failed me in all my life, on my heart, of course also my own—but on the inconstancy or constancy of this part of all my whole I do not find it necessary here to expatiate—and frankly confess that I myself

CHAPTER 1

WARNING (Instead of a Preface)

E VERYWHERE on the Earth, before beginning anything new, it is customary first of all, to pronounce aloud, or, at least mentally, the following words understandable by every contemporary even quite illiterate person—namely:

"In the name of the Father and of His Son and in the name of that Holy Ghost who, if not understood by all ordinary mortals, is, at any rate, understood and beyond all doubt known by our priests and theologians."

That is why I also, setting out on this for me new venture, namely, authorship, begin with these same words and even pronounce them aloud very distinctly and with the proper intonation, with the intonation, of course, arising from the data crystallized in my common presence in the course of my life, those data, which, in general, engender in a man's Being, a quality of intonation manifest of the impulses of "faith," "doubt," "superstition" and so on.

"In the name of the Father and of the Son and of the Holy Ghost, Amen."

Having begun in this way, I ought to be quite assured and to be able to count without any essence anxiety, upon everything further now gliding along, as is said, "on-oil-to-an-Italian-hurdy-gurdy-accompaniment."

I shall begin by placing my own hand—though somewhat injured through a misfortune which recently befell me, yet nevertheless indeed my own—upon my heart, of course also my own, and frankly confess that, for myself, I have not the slightest wish to write; but unfortunately for me, I am constrained to do so by surrounding circumstances, not dependent on my individuality, which have either arisen accidentally, or perhaps have

have personally not the slightest wish to write, but attendant circumstances, quite independent of me, constrain me to do so—and whether these circumstances arose accidentally or were created intentionally by extraneous forces, I myself do not yet know. I know only that these circumstances bid me write not just anything "so-so," as, for instance, something of the kind for reading oneself to sleep, but weighty and bulky tomes.

However that may be, I begin . . .

But begin with what?

Oh, the devil! Will there indeed be repeated that same exceedingly unpleasant and highly strange sensation which it befell me to experience when about three weeks ago I was composing in my thoughts the scheme and sequence of the ideas destined by me for publication and did not know then how to begin either?

This sensation then experienced I might now formulate in words only thus: "the-fear-of-drowning-in-the-overflow-of-my-own-thoughts."

To stop this undesirable sensation I might then still have had recourse to the aid of that maleficent property existing also in me, as in contemporary man, which has become inherent in all of us, and which enables us, without experiencing any remorse of conscience whatever, to put off anything we wish to do "till tomorrow."

I could then have done this very easily because before beginning the actual writing, it was assumed that there was still lots of time; but this can now no longer be done, and I must, without fail, as is said, "even though I burst," begin.

But with what indeed begin . . . ?

Hurrah! . . . Eureka!

Almost all the books I have happened to read in my life have begun with a preface.

So in this case I also must begin with something of the kind.

I say "of the kind," because in general in the process of my life, from the moment I began to distinguish a boy from a girl, I have always done everything, absolutely everything, not as it is done by other, like myself, biped destroyers of Nature's good. Therefore, in writing now I ought, and perhaps am even on principle already obliged, to begin not as any other writer would.

been intentionally created by an outside force, and which constrain me to write not just "so-so" but "weighty-fat-tomes."

And so I begin. But how?

Just in this case, experienced people, "who-know-what's-what," always talk about "being-on-three-horns-of-a-dilemma."

Hurrah! Eureka!

Most of the books I have chanced to read in my life have begun with a preface.

So, I, too, shall begin with something of the kind.

I say "of-the-kind" because in the process of my life, I have so far in general done absolutely everything not as other similar biped beings do, so that, in writing now, I must also begin not as any writer would.

G urdjieff commences The Arousing of Thought with a 123 word sentence that is clearly an inexactitude. It starts with the words:

> *Among other convictions formed in my common presence during my responsible, peculiarly composed life, there is one such also—an indubitable conviction—*

conviction: mid-15c., "the proving or finding of guilt of an offense charged," from Late Latin *convictionem* (nominative convictio) "proof, refutation," noun of action from past-participle stem of *convincere* "to overcome decisively," from *com-*, here probably an intensive prefix (i.e. giving emphasis), + *vincere* "to conquer." Meaning "mental state of being convinced or fully persuaded" is from 1690s; that of "firm belief, a belief held as proven" is from 1841. In a religious sense, "state of being convinced one has acted in opposition to conscience, admonition of the conscience," from 1670s.

common presence: This term is used repeatedly in *The Tales*, indicating a three-centered presence, shared between the intellect, emotions and body.

> *—that always and everywhere on the earth, among people of every degree of development of understanding and of every form of manifestation of the factors which engender in their individuality all kinds of ideals,*

This is a blanket statement: always (all the time, perpetually), everywhere on the earth (without any geographical exception) among people of every degree of development of understanding (no matter how stupid, no matter how intelligent) of every form of manifestation of the factors which engender in their individuality all kinds of ideals (no matter how they act in respect of how they envisage the world (their ideals). To summarize: everyone, everywhere, always.

> *there is acquired the tendency, when beginning anything new, unfailingly to pronounce aloud or, if not aloud, at least mentally, that definite utterance understandable to every even quite illiterate person,*

The passive "is acquired" implies that the action he is about to describe develops naturally. A "tendency" is an inclination or leaning. So while only some people do what is about to be described, the assertion is that everyone-everywhere-always has an inclination to do so. The choice of the word "unfailingly" is curious. The words "understandable to every even quite illiterate person" may seem wildly optimistic, but if everyone has this tendency then everyone must have some ability to understand its formulation.

> *which in different epochs has been formulated variously and in our day is formulated in the following words: "In the name of the Father and of the Son and in the name of the Holy Ghost. Amen."*

We have not been able to confirm Gurdjieff's "that has been formulated variously" by any example from anything other than the Christian tradition. However it is easy enough to find threefold gods in other traditions.

> **Amen:** Old English, from Late Latin *amen*, from Ecclesiastical Greek *amen*, from Hebrew *amen* "truth," used adverbially as an expression of agreement (as in *Deuteronomy xxvii.26, I Kings i.36*), from Semitic root a-m-n "to be trustworthy, confirm, support." Used in Old English only at the end of Gospels, as an expression of concurrence after prayers, it is recorded from early 13c.

The inexactitude is in Gurdjieff's formulation "In the name of the Father and of the Son and in the name of the Holy Ghost. Amen." The traditional Christian formulation comes from *The New Testament* where it is written:

> *Go ye therefore, and teach all nations, baptizing them in the name of the Father, and of the Son, and of the Holy Ghost:*

In more recent English versions of *The New Testament* "Holy Spirit" is preferred to Gurdjieff's "Holy Ghost." The inexactitude is in Gurdjieff's insertion of "and in the name of." Google this and you will not find Gurdjieff's formulation anywhere in English except in the text of *The Tales*.

> **Ghost:** Old English *gast* "breath; good or bad spirit, angel, demon; person, man, human being," in Biblical use "soul, spirit, life," from Proto-Germanic *gaistaz*, German *geist* "spirit, ghost"). Ghost is the English representative of the usual West Germanic word for "supernatural being." In Christian writing in Old English it is used to render Latin *spiritus*, a sense preserved in Holy Ghost. Sense of "disembodied spirit of a dead person," especially imagined as wandering among the living or haunting them, is attested from late 14c.

The Pronouncement in *The 1931 Manuscript*

There are obvious differences between *The Tales* and *The 1931 Manuscript*. First the pronouncement is referred to as "customary" rather than a "tendency." Secondly, the pronouncement is a parody of the usual one, taking a critical sideswipe at priests and theologians:

> *in the name of that Holy Ghost who, if not understood by all ordinary mortals, is, at any rate, understood and beyond all doubt known by our priests and theologians*

And certainly, if one reads modern attempts to discuss or describe the meaning of the Holy Ghost, it sheds very little light.

It seems likely then that in *The Tales* Gurdjieff decided to remove that critical clause and simply draw attention to the Holy Ghost by adjusting the formulation of the pronouncement.

Father, Son and Holy Ghost

Figure 1. shows a commonly published diagram of The Trinity, entitled The Shield of Faith—the name possibly being a reference to *Ephesians 6:16.* where is written:

> *In addition to all this, take up the shield of faith, with which you can extinguish all the flaming arrows of the evil one.*

The diagram illustrates God as a unity, having three aspects that are equal but distinct. The origin of the diagram (originally written in Latin) is

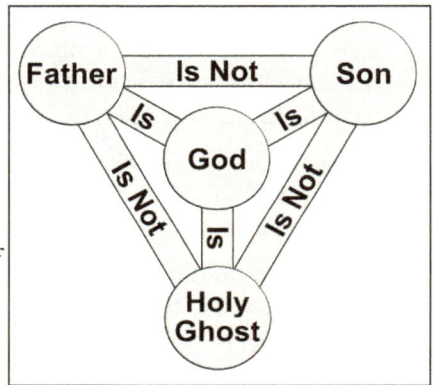

Figure 1. The Shield of Faith

unknown, but it probably dates back to the 12th century. It was almost certainly derived from the Athanasian Creed, a Christian statement of belief that focuses on the Trinitarian doctrine.

Because of the admonition in Matthew 28:19, the trinity pronouncement is a natural part of a baptism, which, if taken seriously, is a new beginning, no matter when it occurs in life. Originally a Christian name was a baptismal name given at baptism. The common act of crossing oneself is also carried out when beginning and ending church ceremonies or prayers.

It is usually accompanied by inwardly or vocally saying: [touch forehead] "In the name of Father" [move hand down to touch solar plexus] "and of the Son" [move hand to left shoulder and then move to right shoulder while saying] "and of the Holy Ghost"[put hands together as if praying] "Amen."

There is little evidence that people invoke the trinity in normal life when embarking on new activities, although priests are sometimes asked to bless

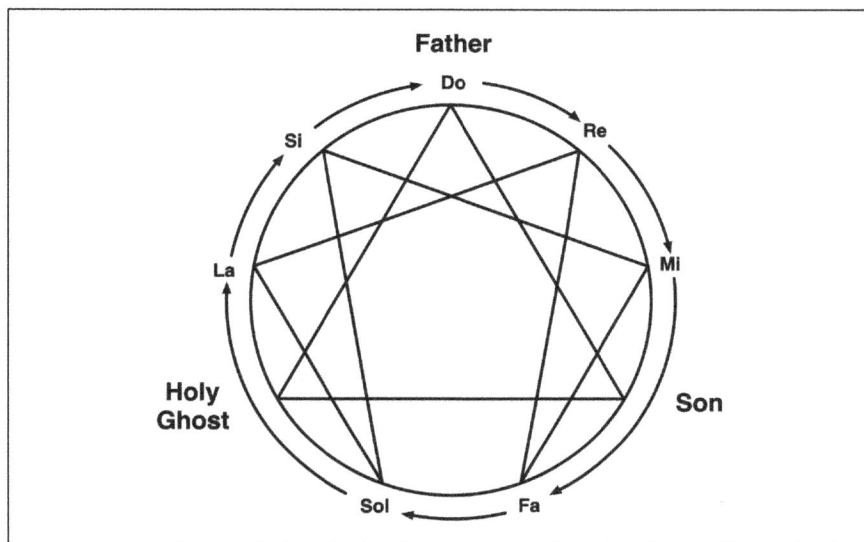

Figure 2. The Trinity Represented on the Enneagram

new houses and the launch of a ship is a formal christening, still accompanied by a blessing in many Catholic countries, but not in Protestant countries.

In The Name of

The expression "In the name of" can be viewed etymologically:

> **Name:** Old English *nama, noma* "name, reputation," from Proto-Germanic *namon*. Meaning "one's reputation" is from c. 1300.

So it could imply taking responsibility or having authority for something, as in "open up in the name of the law" (as I am an officer of the law). Or we could think of it as a prayer, petitioning for the help of higher entities or higher forces. However, it seems most likely that Gurdjieff means for this to be an invocation to ourselves, for the presence of all three centers at the moment that we commence something. We should begin our activity from the collected state.

The Law of Three

By invoking the trinity, Gurdjieff is, in his first paragraph, encouraging us to ponder the Law of Three. From that perspective, Father is active force, Son is passive force and Holy Ghost is neutralizing—the force to which man is largely blind. In a general way, we can translate this onto an enneagram as

79

illustrated in Figure 2. In the illustration we represent only one octave, for the sake of simplicity. In practice a new octave begins at Mi, represented by the point of the triangle labeled Son, and another begins at Sol, represented by the point of the triangle labeled Holy Ghost.

If we think in terms of the structure of *The Tales*, in the place of The Son we would be inclined to place Ashiata Shiemash, a messenger sent from above. And in the place of the Holy Ghost, we would be inclined to place The Holy Planet Purgatory. Then the Father is either Beelzebub as he begins his exile, or alternatively Beelzebub's beatification in the penultimate chapter.

If we consider the three themes of *The Tales* as they play out, we can view the *Objectively Impartial Criticism of the Life of Man* as the Father, the education of Hassein as the Son and the beatification of Beelzebub as the Holy Ghost.

A Wholly Manifested Intonation

With the next paragraph it becomes clear that Gurdjieff is explaining to us how to say the words.

> *That is why I now, also, setting forth on this venture quite new for me, namely, authorship, begin by pronouncing this utterance and moreover pronounce it not only aloud, but even very distinctly and with a full, as the ancient Toulousites defined it, "wholly-manifested intonation"*

The instructions are: aloud, distinctly and with a "wholly manifested intonation." The shock quotes surrounding "wholly manifested intonation" indicate that we should ponder the meaning of this.

intone: late 14c., *entunen* "sing, chant, recite, vocalize," from Old French *entoner* "to sing, chant" (13c.), from Medieval Latin *intonare* "sing according to tone," from Latin *in-* "in" + *tonus* "tone," from Greek *tonos*.

pronounce: This is one of those Gurdjieffian word choices where Gurdjieff is leaning on the earlier meaning of the word rather than its modern meaning. Its original meaning, early 14c., "to declare officially;" late 14c., "to speak, utter," from Old French *prononcier* "declare, speak out, pronounce" (late 13c., Modern French *prononcer*), from Late Latin *pronunciare*, from Latin *pronuntiare* "to proclaim, announce; pronounce, utter," from pro "forth, out, in public" + *nuntiare* "announce," from *nuntius* "messenger." With reference to the mode of sounding words or languages, it is attested from 1620s.

ancient: late 14c., *auncyen*, of persons, "very old;" c. 1400, of things, "having lasted from a remote period," from Old French *ancien* "old, long-standing, ancient," from Vulgar Latin *anteanus*, literally "from before," adjectivization of Latin *ante* "before, in front of, against." The unetymological -t dates from 15c. by influence of words ending in -ent. From early 15c. as "existing or occurring in times long past." Specifically, in history, "belonging to the period before the fall of the Western Roman Empire." As a noun, "very old person," late 14c.; "one who lived in former ages," 1530s. Ancient of Days "supreme being" is from Daniel vii.9.

ancient Toulousites: It is not clear to whom Gurdjieff is referring here. There is little record of Toulouse prior to 118 BCE when it became Roman. That lasted until 418 CE, when Visigoths ruled Toulouse, followed by Merovingian Franks then Carolinian Franks. All were Christian in some form, as was the Cathar religion, which dominated Toulouse for a while in the 13th century. However, it was regarded as heretical by Catholic Rome, which destroyed Catharism in the Albigensian crusade.

Whether the word "ancient" properly applies to the Cathars is moot. Nevertheless, the Cathars chanted famously. It is reported that, as their castle walls were torn down by the "crusaders," they chanted hymns. After their defeat, condemned to death by fire, they chanted hymns as they threw themselves into the flames.

If "as the ancient Toulousites defined it" refers to these extraordinary acts of faith by the Cathars, then the meaning of "wholly manifested intonation" is clear. The etymology of the word "define" supports this.

define: late 14c., *deffinen*, *diffinen*, "to specify; to fix or establish authoritatively." From Old French *defenir, definir* "to finish, conclude, come to an end; bring to an end; define, determine with precision," and directly from Medieval Latin *diffinire, definire*, from Latin *definire* "to limit, determine, explain."

This interpretation is reinforced by the text of *The 1931 Manuscript* where Gurdjieff writes:

> *with the intonation, of course, arising from the data crystallized in my common presence in the course of my life, those data, which, in general, engender in a man's Being, a quality of intonation manifest of the impulses of "faith," "doubt," "superstition" and so on.*

81

Nature and Vivifyingness

In *The Tales* Gurdjieff describes how the ability to "pronounce" these words arises.

> —*of course with that fullness which can arise in my entirety only from data already formed and thoroughly rooted in me for such a manifestation; data which are in general formed in the nature of man, by the way, during his preparatory age, and later, during his responsible life engender in him the ability for the manifestation of the nature and vivifyingness of such an intonation.*

This is the first occurrence of Gurdjieff teaching in an aside. For the reader, this may seem to be a distracting digression from this narrative. However, (as we discuss later) it is a critical element of the writing style Gurdjieff invented for *The Tales*. He employs the technique frequently. Here he emphasizes the importance of being exposed to "wholly manifested intonation" prior to the age of responsibility.

Like a Pianola

The "notions of religious morality" which Gurdjieff criticizes here are clearly those sentimental Christian notions which imply that if one begins an enterprise with the correct "blessing" then its success is assured.

> *Having thus begun, I can now be quite at ease, and should even, according to the notions of religious morality existing among contemporary people, be beyond all doubt assured that everything further in this new venture of mine will now proceed, as is said, "like a pianola."*

pianola: c. 1896, is trademark name (1901) of a player piano, (a piano which plays a tune automatically) from "piano," the ending perhaps abstracted from "viola" and meant as a diminutive suffix (i.e. little piano). The pianola's popularity in America led to a rash of product names ending in *-ola*, especially Victrola and slang words such as payola.

Not the slightest wish to write

In the next paragraph Gurdjieff chooses to describe the circumstances under which the book is being written.

> *First and foremost, I shall place my own hand, moreover the right one, which—although at the moment it is slightly injured owing to the misfortune which recently befell me—is nevertheless really my own,*

and has never once failed me in all my life, on my heart, of course also my own—but on the inconstancy or constancy of this part of all my whole I do not find it necessary here to expatiate—

He does so "hand on heart," but digresses, mentioning his hand injury which he calls a "misfortune." Mid-sentence digressions like this are typical of the style in which *The Tales* is written.

The emphasis "moreover the right one" is most likely a reference to the tradition of swearing with the right hand, which derives from the medieval practice of branding the right hand (palm, or thumb) of a convicted criminal.

> **expatiate:** 1530s, "walk about, roam freely," from Latin *expatiatus/exspatiatus*, past participle of *expatiari/exspatiari* "wander, digress, wander from the way; spread, extend," from ex "out" + *spatiari* "to walk, spread out," from *spatium*. Meaning "talk or write at length" is 1610s.

—and frankly confess that I myself have personally not the slightest wish to write but attendant circumstances, quite independent of me, constrain me to do so

> **constrain:** "to exert force, physical or moral, upon, either in urging to action or restraining from it," early 14c., *constreyen*, from stem of Old French *constreindre* (Modern French *contraindre*) "restrain, control," from Latin *constringere* "to bind together, tie tightly, fetter, shackle, chain," from assimilated form of com "with, together" + *stringere* "to draw tight."

The "personally" indicates that Gurdjieff has no subjective wish to write at all. The reader is thus given to understand that this book and his other books are the product of circumstantial necessity.

and whether these circumstances arose accidentally or were created intentionally by extraneous forces, I myself do not yet know.

In various Gurdjieff-related literature there is a speculation around why Gurdjieff's car accident in July 1924 occurred. The accident and its consequences caused him to turn to spreading his ideas through literature. The suggestion that what befell Gurdjieff could have been "accidental" seems absurd given his level of being (in the sense of his being under the Law of Accident). However, he is stating here that he does not (at the time he wrote the words) know why it came about. It is enigmatic.

> **so-so:** mid-15c., "moderately well," 1520s, "indifferently, neither too poorly nor too well," from so (adv.), which is attested from mid-13c. in the

sense "in this state or condition." As an adjective, "mediocre, neither too good nor too bad," 1540s.

tome: 1510s, "a single volume of a multi-volume work," from Middle French *tome* (16c.), from Latin *tomus* "section of a book, tome," from Greek *tomos* "volume, section of a book," originally "a section, piece cut off," from *temnein* "to cut." Sense of "a large book" is attested from 1570s.

Begin With What?

It may appear that his invocation of the trinity, followed by his confession that circumstances constrain him to write, have already begun the book, but neither of these things say anything at all about its contents. So the question of how to begin is about how to introduce the book itself.

In discussing this he digresses to describe the "disease of tomorrow," an idea which recurs later in *The Tales* and which he frankly admits to suffering from himself—caused here by the overflow of thoughts. But then he writes this enigmatic sentence:

> *I could then have done this very easily because before beginning the actual writing, it was assumed that there was still lots of time; but this can now no longer be done, and I must, without fail, as is said, "even though I burst," begin.*

Only three weeks have passed and yet he writes that he cannot put off beginning the book any longer. He leaves the reader with the question "why?"

A Conventional Preface

There may be virtue in contrasting *The Arousing of Thought* with a conventional preface. Gurdjieff's preface conforms by including the following elements:

- He doesn't state the purpose of the book, but he has stated its purpose earlier by describing the purpose of all three series of *All and Everything*.
- While he does not include any suggestions about how to read the book, he did that in his "Friendly Advice" which can be thought of as the real preface, even though it is not labeled as such.
- He doesn't describe his "fictional work" or its themes, he does refer to the main character of the book.
- He refers to how the book came about.

It fails to conform to a conventional preface in the following ways:

- The preface is by no means short. Prefaces are rarely more than a few pages.
- His "preface" is actually the first chapter of the book.
- He doesn't mention the trials and tribulations of writing the book.
- He doesn't mention his sources or his research process or how long he took to write the book.
- He does not include any acknowledgements.

Hurrah: 1680s, apparently an alteration of *huzza*; it is similar to shouts recorded in German, Danish, and Swedish; perhaps it was picked up by the English soldiery during the Thirty Years' War. *Hurra* was said to be the battle-cry of Prussian soldiers during the War of Liberation (1812-13). Also hurray (1780); hurroo (1824); hoorah (1798). As a verb from 1798.

Eureka: c. 1600, from Greek *heureka* "I have found (it)," first person singular perfect active indicative of *heuriskein* "to find." Supposedly shouted by Archimedes (c. 287-212 B.C.E.) when he solved a problem that had been set to him: determining whether goldsmiths had adulterated the metal in the crown of Hiero II, king of Syracuse.

The 1931 Manuscript

Gurdjieff chooses the analogy of a player piano to satirize the idea that the writing of a book could proceed like clockwork. In *The 1931 Manuscript* he uses a different image:

> *Having begun in this way, I ought to be quite assured and to be able to count without any essence anxiety, upon everything further now gliding along, as is said, "on-oil-to-an-Italian-hurdy-gurdy-accompaniment."*

The hurdy-gurdy is a musical instrument that makes a droning sound. It is played by turning a handle, which is typically attached to a rosined wheel, sounding a series of drone strings, with keys worked by the left hand. It was not a highly regarded instrument, the etymology being from c. 1500 hirdy-girdy meaning "uproar, confusion."

Its sound is akin to the droning of bag-pipes. It is easy to play and can be regarded as a "street instrument" in the sense that it was a beggar's instrument. It is sometimes confused with a barrel organ, a different street instrument. The Italian designation may be due to the fact that it was not unusual for nineteenth century Italian emigrants (to the US, Canada and Britain) to play the hurdy gurdy (ghironda in Italian), to the point where it became a stereotype of that era. The image "on-oil-to-an-Italian-hurdy-gurdy-accompaniment" thus conforms with "like a pianola."

In any case I have begun just thus, and as to how the rest will go I can only say meanwhile, as the blind man once expressed it, "we shall see."

The counterpoint, with Gurdjieff confessing ironically that he doesn't know how it will turn out.

Three-horns-of-a-dilemma

In *The 1931 Manuscript* we read:

And so I begin. But how?

Just in this case, experienced people, "who-know-what's-what," always talk about "being-on-three-horns-of-a-dilemma."

Most likely "three-horns of a dilemma" is a term Gurdjieff invented himself. The sentence is an intentional inexactitude. In normal life nobody ever talks about being "on-three-horns-of-a-dilemma"—we have been unable to find the phrase anywhere else. The term "dilemma" is from Greek, originally meaning two propositions (two *lemmas*). It is a rhetorical device where a debater presents a two-pronged choice to his opponent, neither of which is good. "Two-horns of a dilemma" was first used in 1600.

> **horn:** Old English horn "horn of an animal; projection, pinnacle," also "wind instrument" (originally one made from animal horns), from Proto-Germanic *hurnaz*. Late 14c. as "one of the tips of the crescent moon." The name was retained for a class of musical instruments that developed from the hunting horn. Of dilemmas from 1540s; of automobile warning signals from 1901. Slang meaning "erect penis" is recorded by 1785. Jazz slang sense of "trumpet" is by 1921. Meaning "telephone" is by 1945. Figurative senses of Latin *cornu* included "salient point, chief argument; wing, flank; power, courage, strength." Horn of plenty is from 1580s. Symbolic of cuckoldry since mid-15c. (the victim was fancied to grow one on his head).

Gurdjieff's use of the word "horn" is ambiguous in *The Tales*. He uses horns to signify wisdom and their elaboration (the number of tines) the degree of reason attained, but he also uses them in one part of *The Tales* to indicate cuckoldry. In this instance the horns of a dilemma are the horns of a bull—difficult obstacles to negotiate. Ultimately he edited "three-horns" out of the *The Tales*.

There are "horns" here that he has to reconcile. We can only speculate on what he means. There are enough triples that might qualify:

- Exoteric, mesoteric, esoteric
- Moving centered, emotionally centered, intellectually centered readers
- To impact all three centers
- For it to be possible to be read in three different ways
- Fact, fiction, allegory
- Will the reader be active, passive or neutralizing?

Whatever the intended meaning or meanings, it seems as though Gurdjieff is again drawing our attention to the Law of Three.

-

6

The Warning

"Know and use not the language of grammar, but the language of psychic associations."

~ Gurdjieff

—⁓—

The Tales

In any case, instead of the conventional preface I shall begin quite simply with a Warning.

Beginning with a Warning will be very judicious of me, if only because it will not contradict any of my principles, either organic, psychic, or even "willful," and will at the same time be quite honest—of course, honest in the objective sense, because both I myself and all others who know me well, expect with indubitable certainty that owing to my writings there will entirely disappear in the majority of readers, immediately and not gradually, as must sooner or later, with time, occur to all people, all the "wealth" they have, which was either handed down to them by inheritance or obtained by their own labor, in the form of quieting notions evoking only naive dreams, and also beautiful representations of their lives at present as well as of their prospects in the future.

Professional writers usually begin such introductions with an address to the reader, full of all kinds of bombastically magniloquent and so to say "honeyed" and "inflated" phrases.

Just in this alone I shall follow their example and also begin with such an address, but I shall try not to make it very "sugary" as they usually do, owing particularly to their evil wiseacring by which they titillate the sensibilities of the more or less normal reader.

Thus . . .

My dear, highly honored, strong-willed and of course very patient Sirs, and my much-esteemed, charming, and impartial Ladies—forgive me, I have omitted the most important—and my in no wise hysterical Ladies!

I have the honor to inform you that although owing to circumstances that have arisen at one of the last stages of the process of my life, I am now about to write books, yet during the whole of my life I have never written not only not books or various what are called "instructive-articles," but also not even a letter in which it has been unfailingly necessary to observe what is called "grammaticality," and in consequence, although I am now about to become a professional writer, yet having had no practice at all either in respect of all the established professional rules and procedures or in respect of what is called the "bon ton literary language," I am constrained to write not at all as ordinary "patented-writers" do, to the form of whose writing you have in all probability become as much accustomed as to your own smell.

In my opinion the trouble with you, in the present instance, is perhaps chiefly due to the fact that while still in childhood, there was implanted in

The 1931 Manuscript

In the present instance, instead of the required conventional preface, I shall begin quite simply with a Warning.

Beginning with a Warning will not only not be contrary to those of my already thoroughly fixed principles which have now become, as it were, natural inherencies, but from my point of view—ensuing from the totality of those aims upon which I intend to base my proposed writings—it will be more honest, of course, in the objective sense.

Professional writers usually begin such introductions with an address to the reader full of all kinds of "sugary," magniloquently bombastic what are called "blown-up-phrases."

Just in this alone, I shall follow their example and also begin with an address, but, of course, not with a very, as is said, "mellifluous" one, as they usually do.

Thus . . .

My dear, highly honored and very patient Sirs, and my highly respected, charming, and of course impartial ladies!

Forgive me; I have omitted the most important—and my "in-no- wise-hysterical" Ladies!

I have the honor to inform you that although, with the help of my patron saints and by the permission of the local authorities, and also of course of my "merciless-domestic-tyrant"—a personality, that is, inevitably present in every contemporary household, who has automatically acquired power owing only to the abnormally established conditions of contemporary ordinary life—I am now about to write books, nevertheless, I have not only never during the whole of my life written either books or various what are called "informative-articles," but also never even a letter in which the rules of what is called "bon-ton-grammaticality," prevalent in contemporary civilization, should be observed; and having, in consequence of this, no practice at all in so to say "automatic-twaddle," therefore although I have now to become a writer, I am now in respect of all the accepted rules and you and has now become ideally well harmonized with your general psyche, an excellently working automatism for perceiving all kinds of new impressions, thanks to which "blessing" you have now, during your responsible life, no need of making any individual effort whatsoever.

Speaking frankly, I inwardly personally discern the center of my confession not in my lack of knowledge of all the rules and procedures of writers, but in my nonpossession of what I have called the "bon ton literary language," infallibly required in contemporary life not only from writers but also from every ordinary mortal.

As regards the former, that is to say, my lack of knowledge of the different rules and procedures of writers, I am not greatly disturbed.

And I am not greatly disturbed on this account, because such "ignorance" has already now become in the life of people also in the order of things. Such a blessing arose and now flourishes everywhere on Earth thanks to that extraordinary new disease of which for the last twenty to thirty years, for some reason or other, especially the majority of those persons from among all the three sexes fall ill, who sleep with half-open eyes and whose faces are in every respect fertile soil for the growth of every kind of pimple.

This strange disease is manifested by this, that if the invalid is somewhat literate and his rent is paid for three months in advance, he (she or it) unfailingly begins to write either some "instructive article" or a whole book.

Well knowing about this new human disease and its epidemical spread on Earth, I, as you should understand, have the right to assume that you have acquired, as the learned "medicos" would say, "immunity" to it, and that you will therefore not be palpably indignant at my ignorance of the rules and procedures of writers.

This understanding of mine bids me inwardly to make the center of gravity of my warning my ignorance of the literary language.

In self-justification, and also perhaps to diminish the degree of the censure in your waking consciousness of my ignorance of this language indispensable for contemporary life, I consider it necessary to say, with a humble heart and cheeks flushed with shame, that although I too was taught this language in my childhood, and even though certain of my elders who prepared me for responsible life, constantly forced me "without sparing or economizing" any intimidatory means to "learn by rote" the host of various "nuances" which in their totality compose this contemporary "delight," yet, unfortunately of course for you, of all that I then learned by

procedures of professional writers and also in respect of what is called the "literary-language- of-the-intelligentsia" a complete as is said "booby," or as certain contemporary so-styled "well-read" people would call me, "an-ignoramus-on-the-zigzag-plane-squared"—in consequence of all which, I am not going to write at all like the "Patented-professional-writers," to whose form of writing you are undoubtedly already well accustomed; and I must add that of course in you also, an ideally well working automatism has already been acquired and permanently fixed for perceiving as well as for as is said "digesting," thanks to which "blessing" no individual effort whatsoever is ever required of you.

I particularly warn you about the latter, namely, what I have called the "literary-language-of-the-intelligentsia." Concerning this language it must be said that although I too was taught it in my childhood, and some of my elders who were preparing me for responsible life even constantly compelled me to "learn-by-rote" the multitude of various nuances which compose this "contemporary delight," yet unfortunately— in this case obviously for you—nothing of all I then learnt by rote stuck, and nothing now survives for my writing activities.

And according to the very minute investigations and elucidations of a meteorologist very well known at the present time on the continent of Europe, with whom I chanced to become what is called "bosom-friends" owing to frequent meetings in the nocturnal restaurants of Montmartre, it was not assimilated for the reason that even in my childhood my instinct already contained a certain, as he defined it, "something" which did not permit my Being to absorb this contemporary high-wisdom, and also because, owing to various fortuitous surrounding conditions of my later life, I neither automatically nor semiconsciously, nor even at times, I confess, on principle, that is to say, consciously, employed that language for intercourse with others.

rote, nothing stuck and nothing whatsoever has survived for my present activities as a writer.

And nothing stuck, as it was quite recently made clear to me, not through any fault of mine, nor through the fault of my former respected and non-respected teachers, but this human labor was spent in vain owing to one unexpected and quite exceptional event which occurred at the moment of my appearance on God's Earth, and which was—as a certain occultist well known in Europe explained to me after a very minute what is called "psycho-physico-astrological" investigation—that at that moment, through the hole made in the windowpane by our crazy lame goat, there poured the vibrations of sound which arose in the neighbor's house from an Edison phonograph, and the midwife had in her mouth a lozenge saturated with cocaine of German make, and moreover not "Ersatz," and was sucking this lozenge to these sounds without the proper enjoyment.

Besides from this event, rare in the everyday life of people, my present position also arose because later on in my preparatory and adult life—as, I must confess, I myself guessed after long reflections according to the method of the German professor, Herr Stumpsinschmausen—I always avoided instinctively as well as automatically and at times even consciously, that is, on principle, employing this language for intercourse with others. And from such a trifle, and perhaps not a trifle, I manifested thus again thanks to three data which were formed in my entirety during my preparatory age, about which data I intend to inform you a little later in this same first chapter of my writings.

However that may have been, yet the real fact, illuminated from every side like an American advertisement, and which fact cannot now be changed by any forces even with the knowledge of the experts in "monkey business," is that although I, who have lately been considered by very many people as a rather good teacher of temple dances, have now become today a professional writer and will of course write a great deal—as it has been proper to me since childhood whenever "I do anything to do a great deal of it"—nevertheless, not having, as you see, the automatically acquired and automatically manifested practice necessary for this, I shall be constrained to write all I have thought out in ordinary simple everyday language established by life, without any literary manipulations and without any "grammarian wiseacrings."

The 1931 Manuscript

As a result of all this, esteemed buyer of my writings, though I now intend to become a professional writer, yet having, as you see, none of the mentioned "automatic experience" for it, I am already willy-nilly compelled to disregard— and if you like, I again confess, I will even, as if intentionally disregard—that language and write in the ordinary simple everyday language established by life, without any so-to-say "grammarian wiseacrings."

The importance of the word "Warning" is indicated by the fact that Gurdjieff capitalizes its first letter. It is not enclosed in quote marks and there is nothing unexpected in its etymology.

> **judicious:** c. 1600, "having sound judgment; careful, prudent," also "manifesting sound judgment, carefully planned," from Middle French *judicieux* (16c.) or directly from Medieval Latin *iudiciosus* "prudent, judicious," from Latin *iudicium* "judgment," from *iudicem* "a judge."

> **principle:** late 14c., "origin, source, beginning; rule of conduct; axiom, basic assumption; elemental aspect of a craft or discipline," from Anglo-French principle, Old French *principe* "origin, cause, principle," from Latin *principium* "a beginning, commencement, origin, first part," in plural, *principia*, "foundation, elements," from *princeps* (genitive *principis*) "first man, chief leader; ruler, sovereign," noun use of adjective meaning "that takes first," from *primus* "first" + root of *capere* "to take."

> **willful:** also wilful, c. 1200, "strong-willed," usually in a bad sense, "obstinate, unreasonable," from will (n.) + -ful. From late 14c. as "eager" (to do something). Mid-14c., of actions, "done on purpose, intentional, due to one's own will."

Gurdjieff describes his principles as "either organic, psychic or even 'willful.'" He is clearly referring to principles in the sense of rules of conduct, and these naturally are in three, organic (of the body), psychic (of the mind) or "willful" (of the emotions). The shock quotes may indicate that "willful" in normal usage connotes a negative stubbornness or possibly the act of a strong will, but in his case it may indicate the dictates of conscience.

> **quite honest:** There is nothing unusual about the meaning of honest (free of deceit) but there is about the word "quite." The etymology gives: early 14c., adverbial form of Middle English quit, quite (adj.) "free, clear." Originally "thoroughly;" the weaker sense of "fairly" is attested from mid-19c.

We can presume that here Gurdjieff means "thoroughly honest." He then insists that it is honest "in the objective sense."

Intentional Inexactitude

He justifies his judicious Warning with the following words:

> *because both I myself and all others who know me well, expect with indubitable certainty that owing to my writings there will entirely disappear in the majority of readers, immediately and not gradually,*

as must sooner or later, with time, occur to all people, all the "wealth" they have, which was either handed down to them by inheritance or obtained by their own labor, in the form of quieting notions evoking only naive dreams, and also beautiful representations of their lives at present as well as of their prospects in the future.

This paragraph simply cannot be true. The majority of readers do not immediately experience the vanishing of all their "wealth" and there is nothing to indicate that Gurdjieff or his contemporary associates has such a cast-iron expectation.

"wealth": The quote-enclosed wealth is most likely the "wealth" possessed by the rich man in The New Testament—personality.

And Jesus looked around and said to his disciples, "How difficult it will be for those who have wealth to enter the kingdom of God!" Mark 10:23

Gurdjieff depicts this "wealth" as "quieting notions evoking only naive dreams," (self-calming) and "beautiful representations of their lives at present as well as of their prospects in the future" (imagination).

inheritance: late 14c., *enheritaunce* "fact of receiving by hereditary succession;" early 15c. as "that which is or may be inherited," from Anglo-French and Old French *enheritaunce*, from Old French *enheriter* "make heir, appoint as heir." The meaning of "genetically deriving a quality, characteristic, or predisposition, from one's parents or ancestors" is after Gurdjieff's time. It helps to fix this in the mind when reading *The Tales*. When Gurdjieff uses the word "inheritance" he's usually referring to habits acquired by imitating ones parents or grandparents.

The Judiciousness of the Warning

The reader of *The Tales* is told at the very start of the book that Gurdjieff's intention with this book is:

To destroy, mercilessly, without any compromises whatsoever, in the mentation and feelings of the reader, the beliefs and views, by centuries rooted in him, about everything existing in the world.

He will have achieved part of this goal if he destroys the "wealth" he refers to. However, given that those are his intentions and his "expectation" is that he will achieve this, it is only fair to warn the reader, who is unlikely to expect such a dramatic outcome from reading the book.

The Address to the Reader

bombastic: 1704, "inflated," from bombast + -ic. Meaning "given to bombastic language, characterized by bombast" is from 1727. From stuffing and padding for clothes or upholstery, meaning extended to "pompous, empty speech" (1580s).

bombast: 1570s, "cotton padding," corrupted from earlier *bombace* "raw cotton" (1550s), from Old French *bombace* "cotton, cotton wadding," from Late Latin *bombax* "cotton," a corruption and transferred use of Latin *bombyx* "silk," from Greek *bombyx* "silk, silkworm."

magniloquent: 1650s, from Latin *magniloquentia* "lofty style of language," from *magniloquus* "pompous in talk, vaunting, boastful," from combining form of *magnus* "great" + -*loquus* "speaking," from *loqui* "to speak."

Gurdjieff's satirizes "professional writers" using the hyperbolic words: "honeyed," "inflated" and "sugary." Irrespective of how they address the reader, obsequiously or otherwise, he accuses them as follows:

> owing particularly to their evil wiseacring by which they titillate the sensibilities of the more or less normal reader.

It may be easier to appreciate Gurdjieff's harsh criticism of "professional writers" if one reads the introductory chapter to *Meetings With Remarkable Men*, where Gurdjieff reports his conversation with an "elderly intelligent Persian."

wiseacre: 1590s, partial translation of Middle Dutch *wijssegger* "soothsayer" (with no derogatory connotation), probably altered by association with Middle Dutch *segger* "sayer" from Old High German *wizzago* "prophet," from *wizzan* "to know," from Proto-Germanic wit- "to know." The deprecatory sense of "one who pretends to know everything" may have come through confusion with obsolete English *segger* "sayer," which also had a sense of "braggart" (mid-15c.). The modern meaning is: a person with an affectation of wisdom or knowledge, regarded with scorn or irritation by others; a know-it-all.

It appears that this word was rarely used until Gurdjieff began to employ it.

titillation: early 15c., "pleasing excitement," from Latin *titillationem* (nominative *titillatio*) "a tickling," noun of action from past participle stem of *titillare* "to tickle," imitative of giggling.

Gurdjieff used this word fairly frequently, often as a metaphor for masturbatory behavior.

> **sensibility:** late 14c., "capability of being perceived by the senses; ability to sense or perceive," from Old French *sensibilite*, from Late Latin *sensibilitatem* (nominative sensibilitas), from *sensibilis*. Rarely recorded until the emergence of the meaning "emotional consciousness, capacity for higher feelings or refined emotion" (1751).

The center of gravity of this criticism is that "professional writers" pretend to know rather than know and employ this deceit in ways that excite and ultimately mislead the reader.

Ironic Flattery

Gurdjieff's "sugariness" is laced with irony:

> *My dear, highly honored, strong-willed and of course very patient Sirs, and my much-esteemed, charming, and impartial Ladies—forgive me, I have omitted the most important—and my in no wise hysterical Ladies!*

> **hysteria:** nervous disease, 1801, coined in medical Latin as an abstract noun from Greek *hystera* "womb." Originally defined as a neurotic condition peculiar to women and thought to be caused by a dysfunction of the uterus. With abstract noun ending -ia. General sense of "unhealthy emotion or excitement" is by 1839.

Modern man specifically lacks strong will and patience (which Gurdjieff once described as "the mother of will"). Modern woman is not at all impartial and some are given to hysteria, in the modern sense of the word.

"Grammaticality"

> *during the whole of my life I have never written not only not books or various what are called "instructive-articles," but also not even a letter in which it has been unfailingly necessary to observe what is called "grammaticality,"*

> **"instructive-articles":** The quotes suggest that the meaning should be taken as ironic.

> **grammar:** late 14c., "Latin grammar, rules of Latin," from Old French *gramaire* "grammar; learning," especially Latin and philology, also "(magic) incantation, spells, mumbo-jumbo" (12c., Modern French *grammaire*), an "irregular semi-popular adoption" of Latin *grammatica*

"grammar, philology," perhaps via an unrecorded Medieval Latin form *grammaria*. The classical Latin word is from Greek *grammatike* "(art) of letters," referring both to philology and to literature in the broadest sense, fem. of *grammatikos* "pertaining to or versed in letters or learning," from gramma "letter." The word had a much broader meaning in Latin and Greek; restriction of the meaning to "systematic account of the rules and usages of language" is a post-classical development, until 16c. limited to Latin.

The etymology of "grammar" clarifies the problem Gurdjieff has with modern "grammarians." The words from which "grammar" stems in Latin and Greek indicate a far broader meaning of the word, embracing the whole of philology in Latin and even including literature in Greek. The modern meaning of the word is limited to "the academic formulation of rules applying to the use of language."

Until the sixteenth century, the formulation of "grammar" in the modern sense applied only to Latin. This came about as an effort to standardize. Latin had become the written language of academia, and was extensively used by the Catholic church, even though it was no longer a spoken language. There was a great deal of diversity in written Latin, to the extent it could easily be misinterpreted. The formulation of Latin grammar helped to resolve that problem. Grammar-schools, first founded in the late 14th century were originally schools for learning Latin.

The idea that all languages needed grammatical rules caught on and thus, by the late 16th century, academics began to formulate grammars for other languages, including English.

We can contrast that reality with what the elderly Persian says in *Meetings* which is as follows:

> 'Strange as it may seem to you, in my opinion a great deal of harm to contemporary literature has been brought about by grammars, namely, the grammars of the languages of all the peoples who take part in what I call the "common malphonic concert" of contemporary civilization.
>
> 'The grammars of their different languages are, in most cases, constructed artificially, and have been composed and continue to be altered chiefly by a category of people who, in respect of understanding real life and the language evolved from it for mutual relations, are quite "illiterate".

'On the other hand, among all the peoples of past epochs, as ancient history very definitely shows us, grammar was always formed gradually by life itself, according to the different stages of their development, the climatic conditions of their chief place of existence and the predominant means of obtaining food.

'In present-day civilization the grammars of certain languages so greatly distort the meaning of what the writer wishes to transmit, that the reader, especially if he is a foreigner, is deprived of the last possibility of grasping even the few minute thoughts which, if expressed differently, that is, without this grammar, might perhaps still be understood.

Gurdjieff views the influence of Western grammars as having a distorting and damaging impact on Western writing. The reader is accustomed to reading such works and Gurdjieff "has the honor to inform" the reader that *The Tales* will not abide by that style of writing, because Gurdjieff does not know how to write in that way.

> **bon ton:** bon: French, literally "good" (adj.), from Latin *bonus* "good." It crossed into English in phrases such as *bon appétit*, literally "good appetite" (1860); *bon-ton* "good style" (1744); *bon mot* "good word" (1735), etc.

> **patent:** late 14c., "open letter or document from some authority," shortened form of Anglo-French *lettre patent* (also in Medieval Latin *litteræ patentes*), literally "open letter" (late 13c.), from Old French *patente* "open," from Latin *patentem* (nominative *patens*) "open, lying open," present participle of *patere* "lie open, be open." Meaning "a licence covering an invention" is from 1580s.

The "bon ton literary language" is the language of the intelligentsia, which is how Gurdjieff refers to it in *The 1931 Manuscript*.

In Gurdjieff's Opinion

Gurdjieff writes:

> *In my opinion the trouble with you, in the present instance, is perhaps chiefly due to the fact that while still in childhood, there was implanted in you and has now become ideally well harmonized with your general psyche, an excellently working automatism for perceiving all kinds of new impressions, thanks to which "blessing" you have now,*

during your responsible life, no need of making any individual effort whatsoever.

This will be true of almost all readers. We read with an automatism learned long ago. We read books with minimal attention.

blessing: The "blessing" wrapped in quotes may be a Gurdjieffian pun between the English "bless," to consecrate, and the French *blesser*, to wound. The English "bless" is a native English word, coming from Old English *blēdsian*, meaning 'to consecrate'. This word is cognate with and derives from blood (the semantic link is that consecration back in those days was done with blood). The French *blesser* is ultimately a borrowing from Frankish, coming from Germanic *blaitijaną* (meaning 'to bruise').

More than once we have encountered the suggestion that the English "bless" derives from the French *blesser*. It's a beguiling idea, but we can find no etymological evidence to support it. An alternative interpretation is that the quotes may just indicate irony.

He continues:

Speaking frankly, I inwardly personally discern the center of my confession not in my lack of knowledge of all the rules and procedures of writers, but in my nonpossession of what I have called the "bon ton literary language," infallibly required in contemporary life not only from writers but also from every ordinary mortal.

He sees his announcement, which he now characterizes as a confession, not as confessing a lack of knowledge of how to write—*The Tales* demonstrates that he and his editorial assistants know syntax and punctuation as well as anyone——but that he does not have mastery of the language of the intelligentsia. Anecdotally this statement seems entirely accurate. Gurdjieff did not think in that language or express himself in it.

Ignorance is a Blessing

And I am not greatly disturbed on this account, because such "ignorance" has already now become in the life of people also in the order of things.

"ignorance," ignorant: late 14c., "lacking wisdom or knowledge; unaware," from Old French ignorant (14c.), from Latin *ignorantem* (nominative *ignorans*) "not knowing, ignorant," present participle of *ignorare* "not to know, to be unacquainted; mistake, misunderstand; take no notice of, pay no attention to," from assimilated form of *in-* "not, opposite of" + Old Latin *gnarus* "aware, acquainted with."

The quote-enclosed "ignorance" probably means the act of ignoring. Thus Gurdjieff's confessed "lack of knowledge of the different rules and procedures of writers" is the kind of thing that in those days was ignored (and still is), because few people care.

> *Such a blessing arose and now flourishes everywhere on Earth thanks to that extraordinary new disease...*

It is a blessing to Gurdjieff, in context, not a general blessing.

> **disease:** early 14c., "discomfort, inconvenience," from Old French *desaise* "lack, want; discomfort, distress; trouble, misfortune; disease, sickness," from *des-* "without, away" + *aise* "ease". Sense of "sickness, illness" in English first recorded late 14c.; the word still sometimes was used in its literal sense early 17c.

> *of which for the last twenty to thirty years, for some reason or other, especially the majority of those persons from among all the three sexes fall ill,*

Throughout *The Tales* Gurdjieff refers to three sexes rather than two. This is his first mention of this concept, stated as if everyone knows there are three sexes.

> *who sleep with half-open eyes and whose faces are in every respect fertile soil for the growth of every kind of pimple.*

"Sleeping with eyes half open or fully open" is an uncommon but known phenomenon called "nocturnal lagophthalmos-sleeping." It is unlikely that Gurdjieff is referring to this. More likely he is speaking metaphorically, implying a person in waking sleep who half notices things. If one writes a book, one needs to provide some content, but if it is data acquired while only half-awake it will have little value.

As regards "fertile soil for the growth of every kind of pimple," in general, pimples form from excess oil becoming trapped in the pores of the skin, a condition that is particularly common in adolescence. Gurdjieff associates pimples directly with masturbation. This becomes clear later in *The Tales* as illustrated by the following excerpt:

> *"'For instance, some mama's darling, a young man, inevitably with a pimpled face—and he is pimpled because his mama considered herself a high-brow and thought it was "indecent" to speak of and to point out*

certain things to her son, whereupon this son of hers, not yet having formed his own consciousness, did that which was "done" in him, and the results of these "doings" of his, as with all such young people, appeared on his face as pimples, which are very well known even to contemporary medicine . . .

The Tales p547

Currently, the medical world does not believe that pimples are a consequence of masturbation. The hormones, testosterone and progesterone, can increase oil production which can clog pores, but there is no proven link between testosterone or progesterone levels and masturbation.

In any event, Gurdjieff's assertion makes metaphorical sense in this context, as aspiring authors who have little to offer in their writings are most likely devoted to self-aggrandizement . . .

This strange disease is manifested by this, that if the invalid is somewhat literate and his rent is paid for three months in advance, he (she or it) unfailingly begins to write either some "instructive article" or a whole book.

invalid: "infirm or sickly person," 1709, originally of disabled military men. As an adjective, "not strong, infirm from sickness, disease, or injury", 1640s, from Latin *invalidus* "not strong, infirm, impotent, feeble, inadequate," from *in-* "not" + *validus* "strong."

The manifestation of the disease is that someone becomes an aspiring author if they have some literary skill—skill in the use of the "bon ton literary language"—and have no immediate need to earn money. The quotes around "instructive article" are clearly ironic.

Well knowing about this new human disease and its epidemical spread on Earth, I, as you should understand, have the right to assume that you have acquired, as the learned "medicos" would say, "immunity" to it,

"medico": "medical practitioner," 1680s, from Spanish *médico* or Italian *medico*, from Latin *medicus* "physician; healing."

"immunity": late 14c., "exemption from service or obligation," from Old French *immunité* "privilege; immunity from attack, inviolability" (14c.) and directly from Latin *immunitatem* "exemption from performing public service or charge, privilege," from *immunis* "exempt, free, not paying a share." Medical sense of "protection from disease" is from 1879, from French or German.

Gurdjieff's preference for quoted "medico" rather than physician is interesting. The quoting of "medico" and "immunity" probably indicates a metaphorical use of the words, as what he is describing is not a disease in the normal sense of the word.

> *and that you will therefore not be palpably indignant at my ignorance of the rules and procedures of writers.*
>
> *This understanding of mine bids me inwardly to make the center of gravity of my warning my ignorance of the literary language.*

palpable: late 14c., "that can be touched," from Latin *palpabilis* "that may be touched or felt," from Latin *palpare* "touch gently, stroke." Figurative sense of "easily perceived, evident" also is from late 14c.

indignant: 1580s, from Latin *indignantem* "impatient, reluctant, indignant," present participle of *indignari* "to be displeased at, be offended, resent, deem unworthy," from *indignus* "unworthy."

Gurdjieff employs many words to warn the reader that the book they are about to read is going to have an unfamiliar style and will not be like anything they would normally encounter. On the first reading of *The Tales* in these early pages, this warning is likely to be skipped over and not taken in. However, as the reader advances, it becomes clearer and clearer that this book is not easy to read.

> *In self-justification, and also perhaps to diminish the degree of the censure in your waking consciousness of my ignorance of this language indispensable for contemporary life, I consider it necessary to say,*

censure: late 14c., "judicial sentence," originally ecclesiastical, from Latin *censura* "judgment, opinion," also "office of a censor," from census, past participle of *censere* "appraise, estimate, assess." General sense of "a finding of fault and an expression of condemnation" is from c. 1600.

This is curious. Gurdjieff rarely if ever cared what others thought of him, and thus these words have the character of intentional inexactitude, which should make us pay greater attention. From the context, "waking consciousness" seems to refer to our normal mechanical consciousness.

> *with a humble heart and cheeks flushed with shame, that although I too was taught this language in my childhood, and even though certain of my elders who prepared me for responsible life, constantly forced me*

"without sparing or economizing" any intimidatory means to "learn by rote" the host of various "nuances" which in their totality compose this contemporary "delight," yet, unfortunately of course for you, of all that I then learned by rote, nothing stuck and nothing whatsoever has survived for my present activities as a writer.

rote: c. 1300, "custom, habit," in phrase "by rote," "by heart," of uncertain origin. Possibly Middle English, from Anglo-French, of Germanic origin; akin to Old High German *hruozza* "crowd." Alternatively, sometimes said to be connected with Old French *rote* "route" or from Latin *rota* "wheel."

nuance: 1781, from French *nuance* "slight difference, shade of color" (17c.), from *nuer* "to shade," from *nue* "cloud," from Latin *nubes* "a cloud, mist, vapor" (source also of Latin *obnubere* "to veil," Welsh *nudd* "fog," Greek *nython*, in Hesychius "dark, dusky"). Possibly a reference to "the different colors of the clouds."

delight: c. 1200, delit, "high degree of pleasure or satisfaction," also "that which gives great pleasure," from Old French *delit* "pleasure, delight, sexual desire," from *delitier* "please greatly, charm," from Latin *delectare* "to allure, delight, charm, please," frequentative of *delicere* "entice." Spelled *delite* until 16c.; the modern unetymological form is by influence of light, flight, etc.

The words "taught this language in my childhood" now betrays something unexpected to the reader, as the reader will surely know (and if he doesn't he will soon discover it in the coming pages) that Gurdjieff did not learn English in his childhood, only Armenian and Greek. So the "bon ton literary language" he is referring to is not specific to any particular language; it refers to a way of using words internally and applying that to whatever language one speaks.

The phrase: "constantly forced me 'without sparing or economizing' any intimidatory means to 'learn by rote' the host of various 'nuances' which in their totality compose this contemporary 'delight'" may well have applied to Gurdjieff's upbringing, but probably also applied to our own.

Almost all of us came to use our language in a similar way, being "corrected" by parents and teachers, expecting discourse to observe particular forms, expecting written works to follow particular patterns. We became habitual in this. Gurdjieff claims he did not.

An Astrological Reference

but this human labor was spent in vain owing to one unexpected and quite exceptional event which occurred at the moment of my appearance on God's Earth, and which was—as a certain occultist well known in Europe explained to me after a very minute what is called "psycho-physico-astrological" investigation

The "occultist well known in Europe" is not specific enough to suggest who it might be. At first glance "psycho-physico-astrological" seems like an odd conjunction of words, but star signs are psychophysical categories to which attributes are assigned, so it is not inconceivable that Gurdjieff is simply saying that a noted occultist cast his horoscope.

that at that moment, through the hole made in the windowpane by our crazy lame goat,

The "crazy lame goat" is most likely a reference to Capricorn, Gurdjieff's star sign, whose symbol is the Sea Goat. The hole made in the windowpane, in context, appears to mean the new year, which Capricorn (December 21st to January 20th) "kicks through," or ushers in.

there poured the vibrations of sound which arose in the neighbor's house from an Edison phonograph,

This is a very definitive reference that implies 1877 as the year of Gurdjieff's birth, since that was the year in which the Edison phonograph was invented. (See the discussion below about Gurdjieff's actual birth date and year.)

and the midwife had in her mouth a lozenge saturated with cocaine of German make, and moreover not "Ersatz," and was sucking this lozenge to these sounds without the proper enjoyment.

midwife: c. 1300, "woman assisting," literally "woman who is 'with'" (the mother at birth), from Middle English *mid* "with" + *wif* "woman."

ersatz: "inferior substitute," 1875, from German *Ersatz* "units of the army reserve," literally "compensation, replacement, substitute," from *ersetzen* "to replace," from Old High German *irsezzen*.

cocaine: alkaloid obtained from the leaves of the coca plant, 1874, from Modern Latin *cocaine* (1856), coined by Albert Niemann of Gottingen University from *coca* (from Quechua cuca) + chemical suffix *-ine*. A medical coinage, the drug was used 1870s as a local anaesthetic for eye surgery, etc.

All of this is possibly a reference to the Russo-Turkish War of 1877-78 between the Ottoman Empire and the Eastern Orthodox coalition, led by Russia but including Bulgaria, Romania, Serbia and Montenegro. Russia declared war on 24 April 1877. The Russian army outnumbered the Turkish army, 300,000 to 200,000, but its weaponry was inferior. The Turkish army was armed with British and American-made rifles, which were superior in range to Russian rifles and it also possessed German-made (Krupps) artillery. Nevertheless the Russians prevailed.

Thus we could characterize the midwife as the Ottomans, armed with the latest German artillery, but failing to profit from it. If Gurdjieff was indeed born in 1877, then those events were the backdrop of his birth year and his birth date was 28th December.

> *Besides from this event, rare in the everyday life of people, my present position also arose because later on in my preparatory and adult life— as, I must confess, I myself guessed after long reflections according to the method of the German professor, Herr Stumpsinschmausen—I always avoided instinctively as well as automatically and at times even consciously, that is, on principle, employing this language for intercourse with others.*

As with many, perhaps all, of the names of people (and also places) Gurdjieff employs in *The Tales*, "Stumpsinschmausen" probably has a specific meaning. "Stumpsin" is not a German word, but "Stumpfsinn" is. In *Chapter XXXVI, Just A Wee Bit More About The Germans*, Gurdjieff quotes several lines from a German drinking song, as follows:

> *Blodsinn, Blodsinn*
> *Du mein Vergnügen,*
> *Stumpfsinn, Stumpfsinn*
> *Du meine Lust.*

Roughly translated this means: Nonsense nonsense you are my pleasure, dullness dullness you are my desire. However, as Gurdjieff states, the word "Stumpfsinn" has no direct English equivalent. Possibly the closest English translation is "dullness of mind" or "mindlessness." But if "Stumpfsinn" is intended, then Gurdjieff has deliberately misspelled it as "Stumpsin."

It is unlikely that this is a typo, as Gurdjieff deliberately misspells other names in *The Tales*: Allan Kardec (*p39*) would be Alan Kardec, if spelled correctly, Brade (*p573*) would be spelled Braid (for James Braid), Cognar-de-la-Tour (*p890*) would be Cagniard de la Tour and Seebeck (*p890*) would be spelled

Zehbak (for August Zehbak). It is more likely then that "Stumpsin" is an intentional inexactitude.

Herr Stumpsinschmausen: *Herr* is the German equivalent of Mister. *schmausen* means a feast. If we take "Stumpsin" as "Stumpfsinn," the name would translate roughly as "feast of mindlessness."

Profess: early 14c., "to take a vow" (in a religious order), from Medieval Latin *professus* "avowed," literally "having declared publicly," past participle of Latin *profiteri* "declare openly, testify voluntarily, acknowledge, make public statement of," from *pro-* "forth" + *fateri* (past participle *fassus*) "acknowledge, confess." Professor is from late 14c., "one who teaches a branch of knowledge," from Old French *professeur* (14c.) and directly from Latin *professor* "person who professes to be an expert in some art or science; teacher of highest rank."

We encounter the word "professor" 11 times in *The Tales*, referring either to a German, English or French professor. The meaning intended is probably the conventional meaning.

In the excerpt, Gurdjieff explains what he means when he says "on principle." For something to count as one's principle, it has to participate in one's instinctive, automatic and conscious behavior. Consequently, "long reflections according to the method of the German professor, Herr Stumpsinschmausen" may imply "not using the normal psyche." This is, at least, one possibility.

> *yet the real fact, illuminated from every side like an American advertisement, and which fact cannot now be changed by any forces even with the knowledge of the experts in "monkey business"*

American advertisement: In Gurdjieff's era, neon signs were an innovation, which has since spread to cities almost everywhere.

Monkey business: Monkey business has its roots in the term Monkeyshine. This word was originated in 1832 and meant "dishonorable act;" it was used in the Jim Crow song (Jump Jim Crow) which mocked African-American slaves. In earlier times, parents in England warned their children against bad conduct termed as monkey tricks. The idiom was first recorded in print in 1883 in W. Peck's *Bad Boy*: "There must be no monkey business going on." It's modern meaning is "mischievous or deceitful behavior."

The target of the term "experts in 'monkey business'" is probably academic grammarians. The whole paragraph could be simplified to: I have become a professional writer and I will write this book in simple everyday language.

> *...and will of course write a great deal—as it has been proper to me since childhood whenever "I do anything to do a great deal of it"*

Gurdjieff is stating the fact, sometimes noted by others who spent time with him, that when he learned something new, he learned it to the point of proficiency at the very least. He states here that it was habitual for him to do that in everything.

> *I shall be constrained to write all I have thought out in ordinary simple everyday language established by life*

Most likely, Gurdjieff is suggesting that he will write using the "grammar of associations." While people speak different languages, English, French, German, Russian, etc. their associations always function in the same way. There is an everyday regularity to this which is not associated with the order of words or other academic grammatical forms which insist that meaning must be expressed in a specific way.

It is possible to witness this in the text. For example, in the paragraph we are discussing, Gurdjieff associates to many things: American advertisements, experts in "monkey business," his teaching the Movements, his attitude "to do a great deal of it," and his lack of experience in writing. However, the central meaning of the paragraph is: I have become a professional writer and I will write this book in simple everyday language. And this is only one of several paragraphs which make that point, along with multiple references to the negative aspects of modern grammar.

The 1931 Manuscript

There are a few differences between the two versions that deserve comment. In *The Tales* Gurdjieff writes:

> *I have the honor to inform you that although owing to circumstances that have arisen at one of the last stages of the process of my life, I am now about to write books...*

In *The 1931 Manuscript* he writes:

> *I have the honor to inform you that although, with the help of my patron saints and by the permission of the local authorities, and also of course of my "merciless-domestic-tyrant"—a personality, that is,*

inevitably present in every contemporary household, who has automatically acquired power owing only to the abnormally established conditions of contemporary ordinary life—I am now about to write books...

Most likely the "patron saints," "local authorities," and the "merciless domestic tyrant" refer to elements of our inner world.

In The 1931 Manuscript it is clearer what Gurdjieff means by "bon ton literary language," because he refers to it as "bon ton grammaticality." He writes:

to whose form of writing you are undoubtedly already well accustomed; and I must add that of course in you also, an ideally well working automatism has already been acquired and permanently fixed for perceiving as well as for as is said "digesting,"

"automatic-twaddle," twaddle: "silly talk, prosy nonsense," 1782, probably from *twattle* (1550s), of obscure origin. Gurdjieff characterizes western writing as being both automatic and nonsense.

"booby": "stupid person," 1590s, from Spanish *bobo* "stupid person," also used of various ungainly seabirds, probably from Latin *balbus* "stammering."

"well-read": The quotes probably indicate irony—having read a great deal does not mean that the reading has been done well.

"an-ignoramus-on-the-zigzag-plane-squared": The zigzag-plane-squared may suggest that "well-read" readers will not be likely to tolerate Gurdjieff's sentences, which often include sharp digressions. The "zigzag" is possibly a reference to one of Gurdjieff's idiots, the zigzag idiot, about whom Gurdjieff would say "he has five Fridays in a week." (This possibly comes from a Russian idiom, when someone is described as having "seven Fridays in a week." The sense of this was that they were inconstant, changing decisions, failing to fulfill promises, going back on their word and so on.)

And according to the very minute investigations and elucidations of a meteorologist very well known at the present time on the continent of Europe, with whom I chanced to become what is called "bosom-friends" owing to frequent meetings in the nocturnal restaurants of Montmartre, it was not assimilated for the reason that even in my childhood my instinct already contained a certain, as he defined it, "something" which did not permit my Being to absorb this contemporary high-wisdom, and also because, owing to various

> *fortuitous surrounding conditions of my later life, I neither*
> *automatically nor semiconsciously, nor even at times, I confess, on*
> *principle, that is to say, consciously, employed that language for*
> *intercourse with others.*

> **minute:** early 15c., "chopped small," from Latin *minutus* "little, small,
> minute," past participle of *minuere* "to lessen, diminish." Meaning "very
> small in size or degree" is attested from 1620s.

> **meteorologist:** 1620s. Earlier was meteorologician (1570s). Greek
> *meteorologos* meant "one who deals with celestial phenomena," hence
> astrologer or astronomer.

"Very minute investigations and elucidations of a meteorologist" is a curious
word choice. The meteorologist is an astrologist (as is clear from *The Tales*)
rather than any kind of weather man. Minute investigations and elucidations
may thus refer to precise astrological investigations.

> **"bosom friend":** This term is said to originate in the Latin phrase "sodalis
> pectoris" which means "a companion of the soul." The Romans believed
> that the heart and the chest were the seat of the soul.

Gurdjieff's Actual Birth Date?

In his book, *A New Life*, Paul Beekman Taylor provides an extensive analysis
of what Gurdjieff's birth date may be:

All the documentary evidence, from Georgian and Armenian records, suggest
that Gurdjieff was born in 1877. Records from Alexandrapol (now called
Gumri) suggest that his father, Ivan, was born in 1847. His 1920 Armenian
passport, the 1923 and 1931 French census all list his date of birth as 28
December 1877. His brother, Dimitri's birth year in the 1931 census is given as
1880. Gurdjieff's identification papers shown to immigration authorities in
New York in 1924 indicated 1877 as his year of birth. The 1930 United States
census indicates the same. His German Person Enbeschreibung of 1934 has 28
December 1877.

The only reason there is any question about it is that, on several occasions in
conversation, Gurdjieff indicated 1866 as his birth date—a difference of 11
years. This is supported by some of the content of *Meetings With Remarkable
Men*, which is supposedly autobiographical—however, Gurdjieff would not
have had any problem with changing dates to fit his literary purpose.

As for the date itself, Gurdjieff never celebrated 28th December as his birthday,
preferring instead to celebrate on January 1st or January 13th.

While the passage we've analyzed clearly indicates 1877 (and December 1877 at that, since the Edison phonograph needed to have been invented and the Russo-Turkish war needed to be in progress), it confirms nothing definite in respect of Gurdjieff's actual birth date.

It is also worth noting that 1866 is not the only other candidate. On the back of the book sleeve of the first edition of *The Tales*, Gurdjieff's birth year is given as 1872.

The Grammar of Associations

Gurdjieff takes great pains to explain that *The Tales* is not written according to the normal grammatical form that other books have. The following text from *Gurdjieff's America: Mediating the Miraculous* by Paul Beekman Taylor may help to explain the implications of this.

> *Orage carefully explained the difficulties of a verbal representation of the teaching in a language other than Gurdjieff's own. To translate Gurdjieff's scientific and psychological vocabularies, Orage insisted on the non-autonomy of any given word, for its meaning is limited by the associations it arouses in its hearer or reader, because meaning is relative to audience.*

"Meaning is relative to audience" may seem a bewildering idea given that we tend to assume that the written word is objective and by implication has the same meaning for all who hear. Nevertheless, it is not the case. Audiences are collectively and individually subjective.

> *"Each word we use has only the meaning we, by accidents of our experience, give it," he said. "One's vocabulary is an anthology of associations."*

Orage's assertion would be incorrect if, whenever we encountered a new word, we rushed to the dictionary and fixed its meaning from the definition we found in the dictionary, which would enable us to remove any contextual associations we had made from the situation in which we encountered it. But nobody does that. We accept new words into our vocabulary on hearing them and we deduce or guess their meaning from the context. We very rarely resort to a dictionary. Thus the meaning we give to a word evolves entirely from our subjective associations. It is commonly the case then that even two people from very similar backgrounds misunderstand one another.

> *This simple linguistic axiom, now known among linguists as "relevance theory," incited Gurdjieff to coin words that carry no*

adherent associations, even if the sound of a word may have inherent semantic associations for some.

Orage's explanation is helpful. It is clear from anecdotal reports and from the evidence of the text that Gurdjieff was very particular in the selection of words, to the point where it makes practical sense to assume that he (with the help of Orage) selected every one.

I say "for some" because an axiom of General Linguistics is that there is no psychological relationship between sounds and meanings.

There is clearly a relationship between sound and meaning with words like "buzz" or "hum" that are onomatopoeiaic— but they are the exception.

Orage explained that other Gurdjieffian words (many of which Orage himself selected in his translation) are liable to carry inherent associations into new contexts. So "moonshine" (a distilled alcohol produced illicitly to avoid tax) is a term used by Gurdjieff to identify specious scientific assertions and certain religious and ethical pronouncements. Gurdjieff's term "wiseacring," borrowed from Dutch, indicates vapid philosophising.

There are a whole host of techniques, identified in *To Fathom The Gist Volumes I and II* and described in brief at the beginning of this book, which Gurdjieff uses in order to combat the influence of our subjective associations.

The importance of word-sense to Orage prompted him to suggest a psychology of language for his listeners. "There is a grammar of associations," he explained, "a verbal thought is only a word pattern."

It may help to spend some time considering this: "A verbal thought is only a word pattern." Certainly we think in words, and we tend to speak our thoughts. For example, someone asks us to take a look at a painting and, after a little thought we say "I do not particularly like it." We have given some attention to the painting and formulated an attitude to it. Our spoken words are just a pattern of sound that we have most likely used many times, which corresponds to our reaction to the painting. Our reaction to the painting will have, most probably, been driven by a series of associations invoked by looking at the painting. There are many possible sources for our dislike of the painting, all of which are associations: the colors are off-putting to me, the composition feels odd, it reminds me of a sad event in my life. Whatever the situation, the underlying meaning of "I do not particularly like it" comes from such associations.

"Formal thought can be reproduced in a suggestive way only in words. Formal thought is thinking something, not thinking about something.

Formal thought is constating. We may propose arguments as to why the painting lacks merit. In order not to seem "shallow" we may even invent spurious reasons as to why we dislike the painting. Our explanation of our opinion will appear as if it were, and may even be, a train of logically considered thought.

"There are three modes of speech. First is the expression of one's subjective state; that is, an instinctive verbalization. Then there is emotional utterance, a motion outward; and finally evocative discourse, voice outward."

This is a different way of saying that speech can come from the moving/instinctive center, or from the emotional center, or from the intellectual center. And, of course, it can pass from one center to another in mid-sentence. We can also think of the associations arising from these three centers as driving what is actually said. The meaning of what is said comes from the associations.

Orage wanted his audience to realize that language, like other modes of expression, is largely a habit devoid of precision of meaning. He cited the current phrase "I'm crazy about it," as merely an expression of moderate interest, and "I love it" as expressing moderate pleasure.

We have little doubt that *The Tales* was written by Gurdjieff using a "grammar of associations." It certainly appears that Gurdjieff's sentences, paragraphs and even sequences of paragraphs are arranged according to associations—most likely useful associations he wishes to us to acquire and use practically.

7

In Which Language to Write

"The highest aim of man is to be cunning."

~ Gurdjieff

But the pot is not yet full! . . . For I have not yet decided the most important question of all—in which language to write.

Although I have begun to write in Russian, nevertheless, as the wisest of the wise, Mullah Nassr Eddin, would say, in that language you cannot go far.

(Mullah Nassr Eddin, or as he is also called, Hodja Nassr Eddin, is, it seems, little known in Europe and America, but he is very well known in all countries of the continent of Asia; this legendary personage corresponds to the American Uncle Sam or the German Till Eulenspiegel. Numerous tales popular in the East, akin to the wise sayings, some of long standing and others newly arisen, were ascribed and are still ascribed to this Nassr Eddin.)

The Russian language, it cannot be denied, is very good. I even like it, but . . . only for swapping anecdotes and for use in referring to someone's parentage.

The Russian language is like the English, which language is also very good, but only for discussing in "smoking rooms," while sitting on an easy chair with legs outstretched on another, the topic of Australian frozen meat or, sometimes, the Indian question.

Both these languages are like the dish which is called in Moscow "Solianka," and into which everything goes except you and me, in fact everything you wish, and even the "after-dinner Cheshma"* of Scheherazade.

[* Cheshma means veil.]

It must also be said that owing to all kinds of accidentally and perhaps not accidentally formed conditions of my youth, I have had to learn, and moreover very seriously and of course always with self-compulsion, to speak, read, and write a great many languages, and to such a degree of fluency, that if, in following this profession unexpectedly forced on me by Fate, I decided not to take advantage of the "automatism" which is acquired by practice, then I could perhaps write in any one of them.

The 1931 Manuscript

But the pot is not yet full. For I have not yet decided the most important item of all—in which language to write.

Although I have began to write in Russian, nevertheless as the wisest of the wise, Mullah Nassr Eddin* would say, in that language "you-cannot-go-far."

(Mullah Nassr Eddin, or as he is also called, Hodja Nassr Eddin, is, it seems, little known in Europe and America, but he is very well known in all the countries of the continent of Asia. This legendary personage corresponds somewhat to the German Till Eulenspiegel. Numerous tales popular in the East, akin to wise sayings, are ascribed to this Nassr Eddin; and various witticisms, some of long standing and others newly arisen, still continue to be ascribed to him also.)

I recalled this saying from among the many "infallible" and "indisputable" sayings of that, in my opinion, universal teacher, the wisest of all the terrestrial sages, one whom I particularly esteem, and one who, again, of course, in my opinion, ought to be esteemed and respected by everybody without exception—Mullah Nassr Eddin—and I have set it down at this point in my Warning, because of my proposed subsequent writings I intend often to touch upon philological questions also.

The said Russian language is, it cannot be denied, very good. I even like it, but . . . only for swapping anecdotes in the cooling room of that "Hamman" of mine, which I especially constructed on a spot in that place which by the Will of Fate has become my refuge, like a second "native-land."

The Russian language is like the English, which language is also very good . . . for discussing on the easy sofas of what are called "smoking-rooms," the topic of "Australian-frozen-meat" or, sometimes, the "Indian question."

Both these languages are like the dish which is called in Moscow "Solianka," into which everything goes, dear buyer of my wiseacring, except just you and me. I think I might as well say here also that although the surrounding circumstances and conditions of my life during both my preparatory age and also my maturity have been such that I have had to speak, read and write in many languages, yet circumstances have so fallen out that in recent years I have had practice mostly in Russian and in Armenian.

I can now write in either of these languages with ease, but to my pained regret, the niceties of philosophical questions cannot be expressed in Russian, while, to the misfortune to all contemporary Armenians, although this is possible in Armenian, it has now become quite impossible to employ

But if I set out to use judiciously this automatically acquired automatism which has become easy from long practice, then I should have to write either in Russian or in Armenian, because the circumstances of my life during the last two or three decades have been such that I have had for intercourse with others to use, and consequently to have more practice in, just these two languages and to acquire an automatism in respect to them.

O the dickens! . . . Even in such a case, one of the aspects of my peculiar psyche, unusual for the normal man, has now already begun to torment the whole of me.

And the chief reason for this unhappiness of mine in my almost already mellow age, results from the fact that since childhood there was implanted in my peculiar psyche, together with numerous other rubbish also unnecessary for contemporary life, such an inherency as always and in everything automatically enjoins the whole of me to act only according to popular wisdom.

In the present case, as always in similar as yet indefinite life cases, there immediately comes to my brain—which is for me, constructed unsuccessfully to the point of mockery—and is now as is said, "running through" it that saying of popular wisdom which existed in the life of people of very ancient times, and which has been handed down to our day formulated in the following words: "every stick always has two ends."

In trying first to understand the basic thought and real significance hidden in this strange verbal formulation, there must, in my opinion, first of all arise in the consciousness of every more or less sane-thinking man the supposition that, in the totality of ideas on which is based and from which must flow a sensible notion of this saying, lies the truth, cognized by people for centuries, which affirms that every cause occurring in the life of man, from whatever phenomenon it arises, as one of two opposite effects of other causes, is in its turn obligatorily molded also into two quite opposite effects, as for instance: if "something" obtained from two different causes engenders light, then it must inevitably engender a phenomenon opposite to it, that is to say, darkness; or a factor engendering in the organism of a living creature an impulse of palpable satisfaction also engenders without fail non-satisfaction, of course also palpable, and so on and so forth, always and in everything.

Adopting in the same given instance this popular wisdom formed by centuries and expressed by a stick, which, as was said, indeed has two ends,

that language for contemporary questions.

In my early youth, when I first became interested in and was much absorbed in philological questions, I preferred the Armenian language above all others I spoke. This language was then my favorite chiefly because it was original and had nothing in common with the neighboring languages, of which there is today an innumerable host.

All of its tonalities were peculiar to it alone, and according to my understanding then, based of course, as is characteristic of young people who have not yet tasted the "delights-of-life," upon the impulses of "self-imagining," "self-enthusing," "self-puffing- up" and so on, it responded perfectly to the psyche of the people composing that nation.

one end of which is considered good and the other bad, then if I use the aforesaid automatism which was acquired in me thanks only to long practice, it will be for me personally of course very good, but according to this saying, there must result for the reader just the opposite; and what the opposite of good is, even every non-possessor of hemorrhoids must very easily understand.

Briefly, if I exercise my privilege and take the good end of the stick, then the bad end must inevitably fall "on the reader's head."

This may indeed happen, because in Russian the so to say "niceties" of philosophical questions cannot be expressed, which questions I intend to touch upon in my writings also rather fully, whereas in Armenian, although this is possible, yet to the misfortune of all contemporary Armenians, the employment of this language for contemporary notions has now already become quite impracticable.

In order to alleviate the bitterness of my inner hurt owing to this, I must say that in my early youth, when I became interested in and was greatly taken up with philological questions, I preferred the Armenian language to all others I then spoke, even to my native language.

This language was then my favorite chiefly because it was original and had nothing in common with the neighboring or kindred languages.

As the learned "philologists" say, all of its tonalities were peculiar to it alone, and according to my understanding even then, it corresponded perfectly to the psyche of the people composing that nation.

But the change I have witnessed in that language during the last thirty or forty years has been such, that instead of an original independent language coming to us from the remote past, there has resulted and now exists one, which though also original and independent, yet represents, as might be said, a "kind of clownish potpourri of languages," the totality of the consonances of which, falling on the ear of a more or less conscious and understanding listener, sounds just like the "tones" of Turkish, Persian, French, Kurd, and Russian words and still other "indigestible" and inarticulate noises.

Almost the same might be said about my native language, Greek, which I spoke in childhood and, as might be said, the "taste of the automatic associative power of which" I still retain. I could now, I dare say, express anything I wish in it, but to employ it for writing is for me impossible, for the simple and rather comical reason that someone must transcribe my

The 1931 Manuscript

But I have witnessed during the last thirty or forty years, such a change in that language, that instead of an original independent language, there has resulted and now exists—although similarly original and independent— what might be defined as a "kind-of-motley-pot-pourri-of-languages," the totality of whose consonances, falling on the ear of a more or less conscious listener, rings just like the tones of Turkish, Persian, Kurd, French and Russian words, together with various other completely "indigestible" inarticulate noises.

As for my native language, namely, the Greek which I spoke in childhood, and as might be said, the "taste-of-the-automatic-associative-power-of-which" I still retain, I could now, I dare say, express anything I wish in it, but I cannot employ it for writing, for the following for me very serious reasons.

For must not someone transcribe my writings and translate them into the writings and translate them into the other languages. And who can do this?

It could assuredly be said that even the best expert of modern Greek would understand simply nothing of what I should write in the native language I assimilated in childhood, because, my dear "compatriots," as they might be called, being also inflamed with the wish at all costs to be like the representatives of contemporary civilization also in their conversation, have during these thirty or forty years treated my dear native language just as the Armenians, anxious to become Russian intelligentsia, have treated theirs.

That Greek language, the spirit and essence of which were transmitted to me by heredity, and the language now spoken by contemporary Greeks, are as much alike as, according to the expression of Mullah Nassr Eddin, "a nail is like a requiem."

What is now to be done?

Ah . . . me! Never mind, esteemed buyer of my wiseacrings. If only there be plenty of French armagnac and "Khaizarian bastourma," I shall find a way out of even this difficult situation.

I am an old hand at this.

In life, I have so often got into difficult situations and out of them, that this has become almost a matter of habit for me.

Meanwhile in the present case, I shall write partly in Russian and partly in Armenian, the more readily because among those people always "hanging around" me there are several who "cerebrate" more or less easily in both these languages, and I meanwhile entertain the hope that they will be able to transcribe and translate from these languages fairly well for me.

In any case I again repeat—in order that you should well remember it, but not as you are in the habit of remembering other things and on the basis of which are accustomed to keeping your word of honor to others or to yourself—that no matter what language I shall use, always and in everything, I shall avoid what I have called the "bon ton literary language."

In this respect, the extraordinarily curious fact and one even in the highest degree worthy of your love of knowledge, perhaps even higher than your usual conception, is that from my earliest childhood, that is to say, since the birth in me of the need to destroy birds' nests, and to tease my friends' sisters, there arose in my, as the ancient theosophists called it, "planetary body," and moreover, why I don't know, chiefly in the "right language I desire? And who can do this?

Even the most learned-philologist of modern Greek would understand simply nothing of what I should write in the native language I assimilated in childhood, because my dear compatriots being also inflamed with the wish at all costs to be like the representatives of contemporary civilization also in their conversation have, as a consequence, in the mentioned flow of time, treated my dear native language just as the Armenians, anxious to become Russian intelligentsia, have treated theirs.

That Greek language, the spirit and essence of which were transmitted to me by heredity, and the language now spoken by contemporary Greeks, are as much alike, as, according to the expression of Mullah Nassr Eddin, "a-nail-is-like-a-requiem."

What is to be done?

Eh . . . Eh . . . Ekh! Never mind, esteemed buyer of my writings. If only there be plenty of French "Armagnac" and "Khaizarian-bastourma"—I shall find a way out of even this difficult situation.

I am an old hand at this!

During the period of the process of my life, I have so many times got into difficult situations and out of them, that this has for me become almost a matter of habit. In the present case, I shall meanwhile write partly in Russian and partly, where it is necessary, so to say, to "philosophize," in Armenian, the more readily because there are people near to me and always at hand who "cerebrate" more or less in both languages, and I entertain the hope that they will be able to transcribe and translate from these languages fairly well for me.

But, of course, whatever language I use, you must know that I shall always disregard the aforesaid "bon-ton-language." Why from my earliest childhood I have always disliked this "language-of-the-intelligentsia" I do not know—apparently simply because at the moment of my appearance here below there was being played in our neighbor's house a "phonograph" and at the same time the "midwife" had in her mouth a lozenge dipped in cocaine.

While still a youth, I felt that the whole of my, as the ancient Theosophists called it, "planetary-body," and moreover—why I don't half," an instinctively involuntary sensation, which right up to that period of my life when I became a teacher of dancing, was gradually formed into a definite feeling, and then, when thanks to this profession of mine I came in contact with many people of different "types," there began to arise in me also the conviction with what is called my "mind," that these languages are compiled by people, or rather "grammarians," who are in respect of knowledge of the given language exactly similar to those biped animals whom the esteemed Mullah Nassr Eddin characterizes by the words: "All they can do is to wrangle with pigs about the quality of oranges."

This kind of people among us who have been turned into, so to say, "moths" destroying the good prepared and left for us by our ancestors and by time, have not the slightest notion and have probably never even heard of the screamingly obvious fact that, during the preparatory age, there is acquired in the brain functioning of every creature, and of man also, a particular and definite property, the automatic actualization and manifestation of which the ancient Korkolans called the "law of association," and that the process of the mentation of every creature, especially man, flows exclusively in accordance with this law.

The question: "In which language to write?" ought to be a shock to any reader who thinks about the question. Which author (other than Gurdjieff) would even ask such a question? A ridiculously small number of authors would be capable of writing in more than one language, and any that were would most likely choose the one where they had most practice.

An attendant question is: "What difference could it make?" Only a multilingual author could know, and in the text Gurdjieff provides his considered thoughts on the matter. Clearly he expects the reader to consider this question as well.

> Although I have begun to write in Russian, nevertheless, as the wisest of the wise, Mullah Nassr Eddin, would say, in that language you cannot go far.

Mullah Nassr Eddin is introduced on page 9 of the book, as the wisest of the wise. From this point onwards Gurdjieff uses Mullah Nassr Eddin to provide occasional commentary as if it came from some other general observer of life, aside from himself. Nevertheless, Mullah Nassr Eddin's sayings in The Tales were most likely Gurdjieff's invention.

The 1931 Manuscript
---

know—chiefly with the right-half, and in later years—particularly when I became a "teacher-of-dancing" and came in contact with people of different "types"—I became gradually convinced of it also with my what is called "mind,"—that the so-styled "grammar" of any language is compiled by people who not only in respect of knowledge of the given language are those biped "somethings" which His Uniqueness Mullah Nassr Eddin characterizes by the words "all-they-can-do-is-to-wrangle-with-pigs-about-the-quality-of-oranges," but, who furthermore, have not even any approximate representation of the screamingly obvious fact that during the preparatory age there is required in the brain-functioning of every creature, and, of man, of course, also, a particular and definite property, the automatic actualization and manifestation of which the ancient Korkolans called the "law-of-association," and that the process of the mentation of every "life," including the "life" of man, proceeds exclusively in accordance with this law.

Mullah Nassr Eddin, or as he is also called, Hodja Nassr Eddin, is, it seems, little known in Europe and America, but he is very well known in all countries of the continent of Asia;

Hodja (also khoja): a title of respect usually applied to an Islamic teacher. From Turkish or Farsi.

Mullah Nassr Eddin is a historical figure, born in Hortu Village in Sivrihisar, in present-day Turkey, died in Konya in 1275 or possibly 1285. His tomb is in Akşehir. His fame spread far and wide across Asia, even to China and he is now well-known in the West, partly because of Gurdjieff's influence. In *The Tales*, Mullah Nassr Eddin fulfills a role similar to that of the fool or jester in some of Shakespeare's plays. He is incidental to the action, but makes pithy, appropriate and insightful comments that enrich the story.

this legendary personage corresponds to the American Uncle Sam or the German Till Eulenspiegel.

Uncle Sam: Typically depicted as a thin figure with long white hair and whiskers and dressed in a coat, vest, tall hat, and striped trousers, is a personification of America. He is not usually thought of as a fount of wisdom as the text implies. However, it is suggested that his persona evolved from Brother Jonathan, a rural American wit who used his cunning to triumph over his adversaries in plays, stories, cartoons, and verse.

Till Eulenspiegel: Like Uncle Sam, Till Eulenspiegel was possibly a real person who became a figure of folklore. He was born in Kneitlingen near Brunswick around 1300 and is believed to have died of the Black Death in Mölln, Schleswig-Holstein, in 1350. A chapbook [a popular book sold by peddlers] on Eulenspiegel was printed c. 1510–1512 in Strasbourg. The prankster, Till Eulenspiegel, is depicted with owl and mirror, which is appropriate because "Eulenspiegel" translates to "owl mirror." According to the literature Eulenspiegel's career takes him to many places in the Holy Roman Empire. He plays practical jokes on his contemporaries, especially scatological in nature, and exposes vices and hypocrisy at every turn.

Russian and English

> *The Russian language, it cannot be denied, is very good. I even like it, but . . . only for swapping anecdotes and for use in referring to someone's parentage.*

> *The Russian language is like the English, which language is also very good, but only for discussing in "smoking rooms," while sitting on an easy chair with legs outstretched on another, the topic of Australian frozen meat or, sometimes, the Indian question.*

Gurdjieff draws a surprising comparison between Russian and English. Russian is a Slavic language, the dominant one, and English is a Germanic language, also the dominant one. They employ some different sounds, they have different alphabets, they exhibit distinctly different grammars and sentence structure and they have very few common words. From Gurdjieff's perspective they are alike in their limitations as suitable languages in which to write *The Tales*.

anecdote: 1670s, "secret or private stories," from French *anecdote* (17c.) or directly from Medieval Latin *anecdota*, from Greek *anekdota* "things unpublished," neuter plural of anekdotos, from *an-* "not" + *ekdotos* "published."

Anecdotes are simple stories that rarely involve sophisticated concepts and ironically, etymologically, anecdote means "not published." The reference to parentage comes from the fact that the middle name of a Russian boy or girl

(Ivanovich or Ivanovna, for example) is a patronymic, a reference to the name of the father.

> **smoking room:** In England these were specially designed rooms for smoking in private houses, where, after dinner, gentlemen might congregate away from the ladies to have intellectual conversations. In general they were furnished with velvet curtains and decorated in a masculine way. Gentlemen would often change into a velvet smoking jacket and cap for the purpose (velvet absorbs smoke). This dates back to the 1850s when smoking Turkish tobacco became fashionable.

Gurdjieff describes the posture (sitting on an easy chair with legs outstretched on another) of casual conversation and pontification, rather than meaningful exchange. Wrapping "smoking rooms" in quotes probably suggests that any venue where casual intellectual conversation takes place applies. The "Indian question" and "Australian frozen meat" could easily have been issues of the day that English intellectuals chatted about in the 1930s.

> **The Indian question:** Having conquered India, the British had the problem of administering it. It was the "jewel in the crown" of the British Empire. As well as spices, jewels and textiles, India had a huge population that could and did provide manpower for many things, including soldiering. The Indian question was whether Britain had a right to rule India and whether it could continue to maintain the ability to exploit and administer such a large population (hundreds of millions). It was sometimes argued that Britain was "civilizing" India and had a duty to do so "for the Indians' sake." Such an idea is now laughable.

> **Australian frozen meat:** From the late 1870s onwards, Britain shipped refrigerated meat from Australia and New Zealand. Both countries had small populations and could produce far more meat than was needed locally, while Britain's population was expanding and required a good deal of imported food. Shipping frozen meat halfway round the world seemed like an odd and imperfect solution, but it worked for many years.

> *Both these languages are like the dish which is called in Moscow "Solianka," and into which everything goes except you and me, in fact everything you wish, and even the "after-dinner Cheshma"* of Scheherazade.*

> *[* Cheshma means veil.]*

129

> **Solianka:** This is a thick spicy and sour Russian soup. It is the kind of dish to which leftovers are added. So, aside from the main ingredients, everything else you can find in the kitchen can go in.

The metaphor of Solianka makes the point that the English and Russian languages exclude words and concepts that are required for discussing "you and me."

> **Cheshma:** The source language for this is probably Persian. *Cheshm ha* in Persian means "the eyes." It does not mean "veil." However Gurdjieff may be making some implication, regarding Scheherazade, that her eyes veiled her "after dinner" intentions. An alternative for Cheshma is the Turkish *Çeşme* which means "fountain." This seems less likely, because it is less close in sound to Cheshma.

Scheherazade is the main character in *The 1001 Nights*. Her name (from middle Persian) means "noble lineage." In brief, the story is this: King Shahryar discovers one day that his wife has been unfaithful to him. He has her executed and, having lost faith in the fidelity of all women, he decides to marry a new virgin each day and then behead her the following day, so that no wife will ever be unfaithful to him again.

After he has killed many of his one-day brides, Scheherazade, the vizier's daughter, volunteers to become his next wife. When she enters the king's chambers that night, she asks if she might bid one last farewell to her beloved sister, Dunyazade. Dunyazade has secretly agreed to ask Scheherazade to tell a story when she is called and so she does.

The king is spellbound by Scheherazade's first story, but the night is over before she completes it. He asks her to finish, but Scheherazade says there is no time because dawn is breaking and the king spares her life so that she might finish the story. The next night Scheherazade finishes the story and then begins another exciting tale, which she again fails to finish. In this way the king keeps Scheherazade alive until 1000 stories have been told over 1001 nights. At that point Scheherazade tells the king that she has no tales left to tell him, but by then the king has fallen in love with her. He spares her life and makes her his queen.

The story of Scheherazade itself is an allegory. Interpreting the meaning of "after-dinner Cheshma" is not so easy. The implication may be that these languages are even good for formulating imaginary ideas about the inner worlds of "you and me." Whether that is the case or not, the text of *The Tales* attests to the fact that Gurdjieff invented many new words to express concepts for which, we presume, there were no English words, or even phrases.

> *...if, in following this profession unexpectedly forced on me by Fate, I decided not to take advantage of the "automatism" which is acquired by practice, then I could perhaps write in any one of them.*

Fate: late 14c., "one's lot or destiny; predetermined course of life;" also "one's guiding spirit," from Old French *fate* and directly from Latin *fata*, neuter plural of *fatum* "prophetic declaration of what must be, oracle, prediction," thus the Latin word's usual sense, "that which is ordained, destiny, fate," literally "thing spoken (by the gods)."

Gurdjieff states here that the profession of author was "forced on me by Fate." Note that "Fate" is capitalized for emphasis. If we accept this, then we can deduce that his car accident was also fated. He declares that he has sufficient familiarity with a number of languages to be able to write in them, but that he has greater "automatism" in Russian and Armenian.

> *O the dickens! . . .*

dickens: The word "dickens," used by Shakespeare in *The Merry Wives of Windsor* ("I cannot tell what the dickens his name is"), is most probably a shortened form of "devilkins," meaning "little devils."

> *...my brain—which is for me, constructed unsuccessfully to the point of mockery—and is now as is said, "running through" it...*

The phrase "constructed unsuccessfully to the point of mockery," in respect of anyone's brain, is an enigmatic description. Aside from their natural organic development, brains are constructed only in the sense that their neural pathways enable and emphasize some responses over others. Gurdjieff may thus be stating that his responses are unusual. "running through" may be wrapped in quotes to distinguish its meaning from "stabbing" or "impaling."

A Stick With Two Ends

> *...that saying of popular wisdom which existed in the life of people of very ancient times, and which has been handed down to our day formulated in the following words: "every stick always has two ends."*

> *...that every cause occurring in the life of man, from whatever phenomenon it arises, as one of two opposite effects of other causes, is in its turn obligatorily molded also into two quite opposite effects, as for instance: if "something" obtained from two different causes engenders*

light, then it must inevitably engender a phenomenon opposite to it, that is to say, darkness;

Similar popular sayings include: "there are two sides to every coin," or "every cloud has a silver lining."

...if I use the aforesaid automatism which was acquired in me thanks only to long practice, it will be for me personally of course very good, but according to this saying, there must result for the reader just the opposite; and what the opposite of good is, even every non-possessor of hemorrhoids must very easily understand.

Briefly, if I exercise my privilege and take the good end of the stick, then the bad end must inevitably fall "on the reader's head."

Gurdjieff refers to "hemorrhoids" three other times in *The Tales*, first describing them as a characteristic trait of contemporary actors, secondly as a consequence of using contemporary toilets and finally as a characteristic of humans who belong to the middle-sex.

Gurdjieff subsequently describes the failing of Russian as being unsuitable for expressing philosophical questions. He rejects Armenian as impractical for contemporary notions, noting that the language has deteriorated, with these words:

instead of an original independent language coming to us from the remote past, there has resulted and now exists one, which though also original and independent, yet represents, as might be said, a "kind of clownish potpourri of languages,"...

He then proceeds to criticize the recent evolution of Greek, which was his first language, by saying:

...my dear "compatriots," as they might be called, being also inflamed with the wish at all costs to be like the representatives of contemporary civilization also in their conversation, have during these thirty or forty years treated my dear native language just as the Armenians, anxious to become Russian intelligentsia, have treated theirs.

That Greek language, the spirit and essence of which were transmitted to me by heredity, and the language now spoken by contemporary Greeks, are as much alike as, according to the expression of Mullah Nassr Eddin, "a nail is like a requiem."

Most studies of the origin of languages place Greek and Armenian as being independent Indo-European languages dating back thousands of years. Both languages have adopted words from neighboring languages, but have done so gradually over time. Gurdjieff's criticism relates to more recent adoption of Russian loan words (and even the use of whole Russian sentences) in Armenian, and the similar bastardization of modern Greek with words from English, French, Italian and Turkish.

"a nail is like a requiem."

requiem: "mass for repose of the soul of the dead," c. 1300, from Latin *requiem*, accusative singular of *requies* "rest (after labor), repose," from *re*, intensive prefix + *quies* "quiet." It is the first word of the Mass for the Dead in the Latin liturgy: *Requiem æternam dona eis, Domine* .... ["Grant them eternal rest, O Lord ...."]

While the comparison is amusing, it may also be appropriate. It depends on how you choose to interpret the words "nail" and "requiem." You could take requiem to imply "dead," or more precisely, "a prayer for the dead," implying a memory for something that was once alive. "Nail" might imply "a coffin nail," or simply something relevant to productive human activity (the nail is an ancient invention dating back to Ancient Egypt, but became very important when its production was mechanized in the 19th century) or you might even associate to the Holy Nails used to crucify Christ.

What is now to be done?

Ah . . . me! Never mind, esteemed buyer of my wiseacrings. If only there be plenty of French armagnac and "Khaizarian bastourma," I shall find a way out of even this difficult situation.

wiseacre, wiseacrings: 1590s, partial translation of Middle Dutch *wijssegger* "soothsayer," probably altered by association with Middle Dutch *segger* "sayer" from Old High German *wizzago* "prophet," from *wizzan* "to know," from Proto-Germanic. The deprecatory sense of "one who pretends to know everything" may have come through confusion with obsolete English *segger* "sayer," which also had a sense of "braggart" (mid-15c.).

In "Khaizarian bastourma," Khaizarian may be a variant of Khazarian, from Khazaria. The Khazars were a Turkic-speaking tribe. They established a commercial empire in the 6th century CE in the southeastern section of Russia. It survived until it was laid waste by the invading Mongols. Bastourma is highly seasoned, air-dried cured beef, part of the cuisine of many countries that were part of the Caucasus or the Ottoman Empire.

...I shall write partly in Russian and partly in Armenian, the more readily because among those people always "hanging around" me there are several who "cerebrate" more or less easily in both these languages, and I meanwhile entertain the hope that they will be able to transcribe and translate from these languages fairly well for me.

The quotes surrounding "hanging around" suggest irony, since he is referring to some of his pupils. His quoted use of "cerebrate" is surprising, as he never uses this word again throughout *The Tales*. He frequently uses the word "mentate" or "mentation," which has the meaning "mental function" rather than "cerebration" meaning "brain function."

In any case I again repeat—in order that you should well remember it, but not as you are in the habit of remembering other things and on the basis of which are accustomed to keeping your word of honor to others or to yourself—that no matter what language I shall use, always and in everything, I shall avoid what I have called the "bon ton literary language."

Gurdjieff states, accurately, that he is repeating his intention not to use "bon ton literary language," but interjects "in order that you should well remember it, but not as you are in the habit of remembering other things and on the basis of which are accustomed to keeping your word of honor to others or to yourself." This direct criticism of the reader will probably not be noticed in the first few readings of *The Tales*. Nevertheless it is severe criticism, stating directly that we do not keep our word.

In this respect, the extraordinarily curious fact and one even in the highest degree worthy of your love of knowledge, perhaps even higher than your usual conception,...

He is drawing the reader's attention by stating that what he is about to write is not just extraordinary and curious, but important knowledge.

...is that from my earliest childhood, that is to say, since the birth in me of the need to destroy birds' nests, and to tease my friends' sisters,...

He notes that he had a "need" (rather than simply an inclination) to "destroy birds' nests" and "tease his friends' sisters," which was born in him in "earliest childhood." The implication is probably that such "needs" are born very early in life in every boy (and, possibly, correspondingly in every girl). The attention to his "friends' sisters" implies sexual interest. But what does destroying birds' nests imply? While some adolescent boys become rebellious and exhibit antisocial and even criminal behavior, not all do. It is hard to imagine such behavior as a need, and destroying birds' nests seems like an unlikely way of characterizing it. So it may have a metaphorical meaning. In *The Tales*, birds (the raven inhabitants of Saturn, including Gornahoor Harhark and Gornahoor Rakhoorkh) signify the intellect. So perhaps destroying birds' nests signifies the common adolescent behavior of challenging intellectual authority in science and religion.

> *...there arose in my, as the ancient theosophists called it, "planetary body," and moreover, why I don't know,...*

There are occasional mentions of the "planetary body" in modern theosophical writings, although the term is most often used to apply to the body of a planet rather than of a human being. The word "theosophia," meaning "divine wisdom," appears to have been coined by Ammonius Saccas of Alexandria in the third century A.D. We could find no evidence of the mention of "planetary body" in the writings of the Neo-Platonists (ancient Theosophists), whom Ammonius Saccas inspired.

> *...chiefly in the "right half," an instinctively involuntary sensation, which right up to that period of my life when I became a teacher of dancing, was gradually formed into a definite feeling, and then, when thanks to this profession of mine I came in contact with many people of different "types," there began to arise in me also the conviction with what is called my "mind,"...*

The right half of the body is under control of the left half of the brain which is generally deemed intellectual. Gurdjieff describes an involuntary sensation from childhood which evolved into a feeling which ultimately became a conviction. We provide some notes on "type" at the end of this chapter.

> *...that these languages are compiled by people, or rather "grammarians," who are in respect of knowledge of the given language exactly similar to those biped animals whom the esteemed Mullah Nassr Eddin characterizes by the words: "All they can do is to wrangle with pigs about the quality of oranges."*

esteem: mid-15c., from Old French *estimer* "to estimate, determine" (14c.), from Latin *aestimare* "to value, determine the value of, appraise."

grammar: see earlier (*p 99*) for a discussion on the word "grammar" and Gurdjieff's references to it.

Gurdjieff writes:

> *"All they can do is to wrangle with pigs about the quality of oranges."*

wrangle: late 14c., from Low German *wrangeln* "to dispute, to wrestle," related to Middle Low German *wringen*, from Proto-Germanic *wrang-*, from *wrengh-*, nasalized variant of *wergh-* "to turn." Meaning "take charge of horses" is by 1897, American English. The noun is recorded from 1540s.

pig: probably from Old English *picg*, found in compounds, further etymology unknown. Originally "young pig" (the word for adults was swine). Apparently related to Low German *bigge*, Applied to persons, usually in contempt, since 1540s; the derogatory slang meaning "police officer" has been in underworld slang at least since 1811. Sailors and fishermen are said to avoid uttering the word "pig" at sea, in case it should bring bad luck—a superstition perhaps based on the fate of the Gadarene swine, who drowned.

quality: c. 1300, "temperament, character, disposition," from Old French *qualite* "quality, nature, characteristic," from Latin *qualitatem,* "a quality, property; nature, state, condition" (said to have been coined by Cicero to translate Greek *poiotes*), from *qualis* "what kind of a." Meaning "degree of goodness" is late 14c. Meaning "social rank, position" is c. 1400.

The symbol "pig" is sometimes used to refer to man (derogatorily), as in the English saying:

Cats are superior, dogs are inferior, pigs are man's equal.

In *Life is Real*, Gurdjieff provides the following saying:

"A man is not a pig to forget good, nor is he a cat to remember evil:"

While pigs can in general eat most kinds of food, they are rarely fed citrus fruit because it can upset their stomachs. They should thus have little genuine interest in the quality of oranges.

Gurdjieff writes:

This kind of people among us who have been turned into, so to say, "moths" destroying the good prepared and left for us by our ancestors and by time, have not the slightest notion and have probably never even heard of the screamingly obvious fact that,...

moth: Old English *moððe* (Northumbrian *mohðe*), Old Norse *motti*, Middle Dutch *motte*, Dutch *mot*, German *Motte* all meaning "moth." Perhaps related to Old English *maða* "maggot." Until 16c. was used mostly of the larva and usually in reference to devouring clothes, which makes sense as it is only the larvae that devour clothes.

Note that "moth" is a New Testament symbol, which can be found in *Matthew vi.19-20*, as follows:

> *Lay not up for yourselves treasures upon earth, where moth and rust doth corrupt, and where thieves break through and steal:*
>
> *But lay up for yourselves treasures in heaven, where neither moth nor rust doth corrupt, and where thieves do not break through nor steal:*

He continues

> *...during the preparatory age, there is acquired in the brain functioning of every creature, and of man also, a particular and definite property, the automatic actualization and manifestation of which the ancient Korkolans called the "law of association," and that the process of the mentation of every creature, especially man, flows exclusively in accordance with this law.*

Korkolans probably refers to the inhabitants of Koorkalai, the capital city of Tikliamish, which Gurdjieff introduces on Beelzebub's second descent. If that's the case he has deliberately misspelled the word, omitting the second "o." The text of *The Tales* clearly depicts Tikliamish as an intellectual culture and hence it is credible that the Korkolans formulated a "law of association."

The statement that "the process of the mentation of every creature, especially man, flows exclusively in accordance with" association, is worthy of pondering and observation. Earlier in the text, referring to the Greek language, Gurdjieff writes:

> *...which I spoke in childhood and, as might be said, the "taste of the automatic associative power of which" I still retain.*

Without explanation, Gurdjieff states that languages are imbued with "automatic associative power."

The 1931 Manuscript

There are only a few notable differences between *The 1931 Manuscript* and *The Tales* in this section. One is Gurdjieff's mention of the Hammam at the Prieuré.

> *...for swapping anecdotes in the cooling room of that "Hamman" of mine, which I especially constructed on a spot in that place which by the Will of Fate has become my refuge, like a second "native-land."*

The description of Solianka does not include the enigmatic reference to Scheherezade:

Both these languages are like the dish which is called in Moscow "Solianka," into which everything goes, dear buyer of my wiseacring, except just you and me.

In referring to Armenian, in *The Tales*, but not in *The 1931 Manuscript*, Gurdjieff writes:

As the learned "philologists" say, all of its tonalities were peculiar to it alone, and according to my understanding even then, it corresponded perfectly to the psyche of the people composing that nation.

In *The 1931 Manuscript* he writes as follows:

In my early youth, when I first became interested in and was much absorbed in philological questions, I preferred the Armenian language above all others I spoke. This language was then my favorite chiefly because it was original and had nothing in common with the neighboring languages, of which there is today an innumerable host.

Practically, his choice of the Armenian language for some of his writing appears to have had more to do with it having an appropriate vocabulary for concepts he wished to discuss than either of the above plaudits.

Types

When Gurdjieff mentions "types" what he means precisely is unclear, even though he mentions it many times. In *The Tales*, when writing of ways in which three-brained beings "love" someone:

...or because his nose is much like the nose of that female or male, with whom thanks to the cosmic law of "polarity" or "type" a relation has been established which has not yet been broken... (p358)

He also writes:

Love of consciousness evokes the same in response
Love of feeling evokes the opposite
Love of body depends only on type and polarity. (p361)

In describing the "acting" of the Babylonian mysterists, he writes:

Well then, these three learned beings who were thus cast impromptu by the fourth learned being for fulfilling every kind of perception and manifestation, which had to flow by law, of types foreign to them, or, as your favorites say, of 'strange roles,'... (p484)

He adds:

...because the learned beings of the planet Earth of that time were very well aware of what is called the 'law-of-typicality,' and that the three-brained beings of their planet are ultimately formed into twenty-seven different definite types,... (p486)

Later, in discussing Judas, he writes:

when this Sacred Individual Jesus Christ, intentionally actualized from Above in a planetary body of a terrestrial being, completely formed Himself for a corresponding existence, He decided to actualize the mission imposed on Him from Above, through the way of enlightening the reason of these three-brained terrestrial beings, by means of twelve different types of beings, chosen from among them and who were specially enlightened and prepared by him personally.

In discussing "intelligentsics," he describes the following types or categories:

'Bureaucrats'

'Plutocrats'

'Theocrats'

'Democrats'

'Zevrocrats'

'Aristocrats' (p1082)

Towards the beginning of the final chapter he writes:

I—or rather, this time, that dominant something in my common presence which now represents the sum of the results obtained from the data crystallized during my life, data which engender, among other things, in a man who has in general set himself the aim, so to say "to mentate actively impartially" during the process of responsible existence, the ability to penetrate and understand the psyche of people of various types...

And to add to that information, but not to lessen the confusion, in *The Herald* he writes:

...I was compelled to give them all up and to undertake the organization of my own "circle" on quite new principles, with a staff of people chosen specially by me.

I decided to do so mainly for the reason that, meeting then a great number of people usually composing such circles, I had elucidated and established the fact that in such societies foregather generally people of three or four definite "types", whereas it was necessary for me —in order to observe the manifestations of man's psyche in his waking state—to have at my disposal representatives of all the 28 "categories-of-types" existing on Earth, as they were established in ancient times.

The 1931 Manuscript contains a further reference to "types" in the part that discusses astrologers. Gurdjieff writes:

...indicated just what they had to do to their own planetary body at which definite periods of the Krentonalnian movements of their planet—as for instance, in which direction to lie, how to breathe, which movements to make in preference, with which types to avoid relations and many things of the same kind. (p270)

8

Two Kinds of Mentation

"There are two lines along which man's development proceeds, the line of knowledge and the line of being."

~ *Gurdjieff*

In view of the fact that I have happened here accidentally to touch upon a question which has lately become one of my so to speak "hobbies," namely, the process of human mentation, I consider it possible, without waiting for the corresponding place predetermined by me for the elucidation of this question, to state already now in this first chapter at least something concerning that axiom which has accidentally become known to me, that on Earth in the past it has been usual in every century that every man, in whom there arises the boldness to attain the right to be considered by others and to consider himself a "conscious thinker," should be informed while still in the early years of his responsible existence that man has in general two kinds of mentation: one kind, mentation by thought, in which words, always possessing a relative sense, are employed; and the other kind, which is proper to all animals as well as to man, which I would call "mentation by form."

The second kind of mentation, that is, "mentation by form," by which, strictly speaking, the exact sense of all writing must be also perceived, and after conscious confrontation with information already possessed, be assimilated, is formed in people in dependence upon the conditions of geographical locality, climate, time, and, in general, upon the whole environment in which the arising of the given man has proceeded and in which his existence has flowed up to manhood.

Accordingly, in the brains of people of different races and conditions dwelling in different geographical localities, there are formed about one and the same thing or even idea, a number of quite independent forms, which during functioning, that is to say, association, evoke in their being some sensation or other which subjectively conditions a definite picturing, and which picturing is expressed by this, that, or the other word, that serves only for its outer subjective expression.

That is why each word, for the same thing or idea, almost always acquires for people of different geographical locality and race a very definite and entirely different so to say "inner content."

In other words, if in the entirety of any man who has arisen and been formed in any locality, from the results of the specific local influences and impressions a certain "form" has been composed, and this form evokes in him by association the sensation of a definite "inner content," and consequently of a definite picturing or notion for the expression of which he employs one or another word which has eventually become habitual, and

The 1931 Manuscript

From the very beginning on the Earth it has become usual that every man who, so to say, "devotes-himself-to-the-field-of-a-conscious-thinker" should be well informed while still in the early years of his responsible existence, that man has in general two kinds of mentation; one kind, by thoughts, for the expression of which, subjective words, possessing always a relative sense, are employed; and another kind, proper to man as well as to all animals, called by those same ancient Korkolans "mentation-by-form."

The second kind of mentation, by which, strictly speaking, the exact sense of all writing must also be perceived, is formed in dependence upon the conditions of geographical locality, climate, time and, in general, upon the whole environment in which the arising of the given man has proceeded and in which his existence has flowed up to maturity.

Accordingly, in the brains of people of different geographical localities, different races and different conditions, there are formed about one and the same thing or idea, a number of quite independent forms, which in their association evoke in a being some sensation or other which in turn conditions a picturing, and which picturings in their turn are expressed by this, that or the other word that serves for their outer expression.

That is why each word, for the same thing or idea, almost always acquires for people of varying geographical locality and race, entirely different so to say "inner-content."

In other words, suppose that in the common presence of some given man who has arisen and been formed in any given locality, a certain "form" has been crystallized from the results of specific local influences and impressions, and that this form evokes in him by association the sensation of a definite "inner- content" and consequently of a definite image or notion, and he should then employ for the expression of this image or notion some word which has eventually become habitual and subjective to him, then, the hearer of that word—in whose being, owing to the quite other conditions of his arising and formation, there has been crystallized concerning the given word, quite another form of data for the mentioned "inner-content"—will in consequence always perceive and inevitably understand that same word in quite another sense.

This fact, by the way, can with attentive and impartial observation be very clearly constated when one is present at an exchange of opinions between persons belonging to different nations.

as I have said, subjective to him, then the hearer of that word, in whose being, owing to different conditions of his arising and growth, there has been formed concerning the given word a form of a different "inner content," will always perceive and of course infallibly understand that same word in quite another sense.

This fact, by the way, can with attentive and impartial observation be very clearly established when one is present at an exchange of opinions between persons belonging to two different races or who arose and were formed in different geographical localities.

And so, cheerful and swaggering candidate for a buyer of my wiseacrings, having warned you that I am going to write not as "professional writers" usually write but quite otherwise, I advise you, before embarking on the reading of my further expositions, to reflect seriously and only then to undertake it. If not, I am afraid for your hearing and other perceptive and also digestive organs which may be already so thoroughly automatized to the "literary language of the intelligentsia" existing in the present period of time on Earth, that the reading of these writings of mine might affect you very, very cacophonously, and from this you might lose your . . . you know what? . . . your appetite for your favorite dish and for your psychic specificness which particularly titillates your "inside" and which proceeds in you on seeing your neighbor, the brunette.

For such a possibility, ensuing from my language, or rather, strictly speaking, from the form of my mentation, I am, thanks to oft-repeated past experiences, already quite as convinced with my whole being as a "thoroughbred donkey" is convinced of the right and justice of his obstinacy.

Now that I have warned you of what is most important, I am already tranquil about everything further. Even if any misunderstanding should arise on account of my writings, you alone will be entirely to blame, and my conscience will be as clear as for instance . . . the ex-Kaiser Wilhelm's.

In all probability you are now thinking that I am, of course, a young man with an auspicious exterior and, as some express it, a "suspicious interior," and that, as a novice in writing, I am evidently intentionally being eccentric in the hope of becoming famous and thereby rich.

If you indeed think so, then you are very, very mistaken.

First of all, I am not young; I have already lived so much that I have been in my life, as it is said, "not only through the mill but through all the

The 1931 Manuscript

And so, esteemed buyer of my writings, I warn you that I am going to write not as "professional-writers" usually write, but quite otherwise. So before embarking on the reading of my further "wiseacrings," first reflect seriously, and only then undertake it. Maybe your hearing and other perceptive organs are already so thoroughly automatized to the "literary-language- of-the-intelligentsia," that the reading of these writings of mine might affect you frightfully cacophonously, as a result of which you might lose your . . . you know what? . . . your relish for your favorite dish.

I consider it my duty to say, that thanks to oft-repeated past experiences, I am already quite as convinced with my whole being of this possibility ensuing from my language or rather from the form of my mentation, as a "thoroughbred-donkey" is convinced of the right and justice of his obstinacy.

Now that I have given you warning of the most important thing, I am already tranquil about everything further, because if any misunderstanding should arise on account of my writings, you alone will be entirely to blame, and my own conscience will be as clear as the Ex-Kaiser Wilhelm's.

In all probability you are now thinking that, as a novice in writing, I am obviously trying to be eccentric, in the hope of becoming famous and thereby rich. And of course you also think that I am a young man with a pleasing exterior and, as some express it, "suspicious-interior."

If you indeed think so, then you are mightily mistaken. First of all, I am not young. I have already lived so much that I have been through even more

The Tales

grindstones"; and secondly, I am in general not writing so as to make a career for myself, or so as to plant myself, as is said, "firmfootedly," thanks to this profession, which, I must add, in my opinion provides many openings to become a candidate d-i-r-e-c-t for "Hell"—assuming of course that such people can in general by their Being, perfect themselves even to that extent, for the reason that knowing nothing whatsoever themselves, they write all kinds of "claptrap" and thereby automatically acquiring authority, they become almost one of the chief factors, the totality of which steadily continues year by year, still further to diminish the, without this, already extremely diminished psyche of people.

And as regards my personal career, then thanks to all forces high and low and, if you like, even right and left, I have actualized it long ago, and have already long been standing on "firm feet" and even maybe on very good feet, and I moreover am certain that their strength is sufficient for many more years, in spite of all my past, present, and future enemies.

Yes, I think you might as well be told also about an idea which has only just arisen in my madcap brain, and namely, specially to request the printer, to whom I shall give my first book, to print this first chapter of my writings in such a way that anybody may read it before cutting the pages of the book itself, whereupon, on learning that it is not written in the usual manner, that is to say, for helping to produce in one's mentation, very smoothly and easily, exciting images and lulling reveries, he may, if he wishes, without wasting words with the bookseller, return it and get his money back, money perhaps earned by the sweat of his own brow.

than one mill in my life; and secondly, I am not trying to be eccentric nor do I intend to make my career or to plant myself in this profession—a profession which, I must add, in my opinion provides many opportunities for candidates d.i.r.e.c.t. . . . for "Hell," assuming of course, that such people can in general by their Being perfect themselves to that extent—for the reason that knowing nothing whatsoever themselves, they write all kinds of "claptrap," and acquiring authority thereby, they become, of course unconsciously, what are called "automatically-working- factors" for the diminution of the without this already sufficiently diminished psyche of those around them.

And as regards my personal career, then thanks to all forces high and low and, if you like, even right and left, I have actualized it long ago, and have already long been standing on "firm-feet," and maybe on very good feet; and moreover, I am certain that their strength is sufficient for many more years, in spite of all my past and future enemies.

But enough of trifling, old fellow, one must write. Yes . . . I think you might as well be told also about an idea which has only arisen in my brain, and namely, specially to request the printers, to whom I shall give my first book, to print this warning on the opening pages so that anybody may read it before cutting the pages of the book itself, whereupon, on learning that it is not written in the "language-of-the- intelligentsia," he may if he likes, without wasting words with the bookseller, return it and get his money back, which perhaps he has earned by the sweat of his brow.

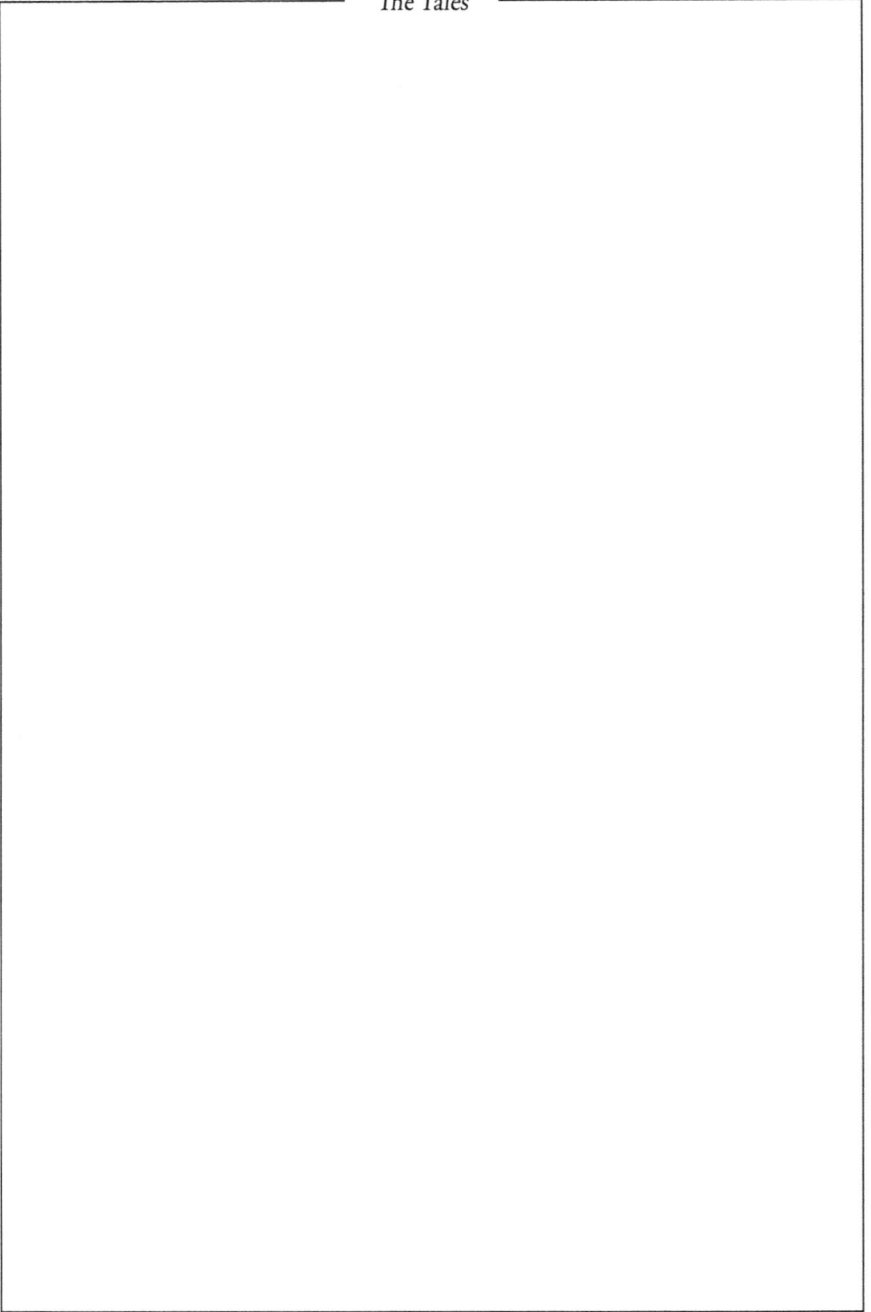

The Tales

While writing and cogitating how to explain this idea to Mr. Printer, there arose unsought in this madcap brain of mine, another idea quite disadvantageous for me personally, namely, the idea to be sure to assign a definite sum of money for the misunderstandings which may arise when the uncut books are returned to the bookseller.

The disadvantage to myself in this idea which has spontaneously arisen in my madcap brain consists chiefly in this; that I shall be forced to take this money from a fund, dependent solely on my own will, free from the advice or disagreement of others, misbegotten busybodies, always around me, and, namely, from what is called my "Crayfish-fund."

Now that I happen to be speaking of this fund of mine, which depends solely on my independent will, objective justice demands that I should not fail, first of all, to praise and extol with an impulse of great affection and sentiment the names of the noble "Uncle Sam" and "John Bull," and then, with an impulse of gratitude, to remark that during several years, genuine sprigs of those names I have just extolled, who for various objective merits have become worthy to rank as "Crayfish-idiots," have hitherto always punctually and even with unction kept supplied and so far still supply this solitary hearth of my, so to say, hopes and expectations.

It must be allowed that by reducing the number of my so to say "crayfish-parasites," who have become indispensable assistants in what has lately become, as it were, a necessity for my recreation, I ought to be able also to provide that sum of money from this fund, but owing to that specific and moreover terrible disease, always chronic and, lately, on the increase among the poor and wretched money-changers, which disease has become well known on the Earth under the description of being "hell-bent," not even such a self-deprivation can save me, because on account of this terrible disease, it has already now become extremely difficult for me to make both ends meet.

Eh . . . Ekh! . . . unfortunate me, hapless victim of a combination of planetary influences at the moment of my appearance here below!

This time also it is already beyond doubt—as it has happened to me many a time before my arrival in Europe—that on account of this altruistic intention which spontaneously arose in me, all the rest of the parts of my entire whole will once again "totally-unexpectedly" be made the "scapegoats." It has always been so; no sooner does an idea arise in my madcap brain, but it inexorably compels the whole of me to carry it out at

The Tales

any cost, as for instance in the present case, to assign without fail the said sum of money, when, in fact, I have none, nor are there in sight any likely "fat-sheep-for-shearing."

The data engendering just this feature of my character, on account of which on all occasions, all kinds of factors for the formation of diverse for me personally "indigestible-consequences" always arise, were crystallized in my common presence from an impression perceived by me in my early youth, thanks to a story I heard about what happened to a certain "Transcaucasian Kurd."

Of course I must not fail to confess here, that it was only recently that I made clear to my pure Reason when precisely these data for my psyche were formed in me and all the details of their crystallization—that is to say, it was only after I had forced myself to spend a certain time punctiliously following all the indications of the Yogis and after I had later thoroughly studied from all sides that perfectly bewitching branch of "contemporary science" now existing everywhere under the name of "Psycho-analysis."

These specific data together with other similar data which constitute and manifest my present individuality, and which had in their formation decidedly nothing issuing from my essence and which were crystallized in my common presence owing only to various fortuitous surrounding conditions of my life, not only became thereafter, for the whole of me for the rest of my life, almost the dominant what is called "initiating- factor" in the begetting of always the same "indigestible consequences," but also, during their, as the learned psychiatrists would say, "gravity-center-functioning," which proceeds in general under the influence of a corresponding association, they evoke in me almost every time the experiencings called in ancient Indian philosophy "commiseration-with-impartial-affection."

Thanks to this feature of my character, on account of which especially in recent years, I find myself already quite incapable of refraining from actualizing in practice every idea, however personally disadvantageous to me, so in this case also, the whole of my common presence will be inexorably compelled to follow this solicitous procedure, merely in order to caution you, just you a person wholly alien to me, against falling a victim to cunning through the effect upon you of the usual "honeyed-words" of the bookseller; I repeat that I do this in spite of the fact that this measure, as you see for yourselves will mean a considerable loss for me personally.

G urdjieff puts a significant amount of effort into preparing the reader to read his book. It's clear that he knows the reader will miss most of what he is trying to convey on the first few readings of the book, even though it is there on the page. The diligent reader will, however, return again and again to the text knowing that they never fully understood the words on previous readings. Eventually the reader will realize that they will need to know more about themselves just to read the book.

> *In view of the fact that I have happened here accidentally to touch upon a question which has lately become one of my so to speak "hobbies," namely, the process of human mentation,...*

hobby: 1400, hobi, "small, active horse," short for *hobyn* (mid-14c.; late 13c. in Anglo-Latin), probably originally a proper name for a horse (compare dobbin), a diminutive of Robert or Robin. The modern sense of "a favorite pursuit, object, or topic" is from 1816, a shortening of hobbyhorse. Hobby as a shortening of hobbyhorse also was used in the "morris horse" sense (1760) and the "child's toy horse" sense (1680s).

The use of the word "hobbies" is ironic. He never happened upon the question of association accidentally as the text claims. There is nothing accidental in *The Tales.*

> *that on Earth in the past it has been usual in every century that every man, in whom there arises the boldness to attain the right to be considered by others and to consider himself a "conscious thinker," should be informed while still in the early years of his responsible existence that man has in general two kinds of mentation: one kind, mentation by thought, in which words, always possessing a relative sense, are employed; and the other kind, which is proper to all animals as well as to man, which I would call "mentation by form."*

It is clearly "inexactitude" to suggest that anything of the kind "has been usual." The "in whom there arises the boldness to attain the right to be considered by others and to consider himself a 'conscious thinker,'" is a curious collection of words. It implies that "boldness" is required of those who wish to be a "conscious thinker." "Bold" means "brave, confident, strong," both in current usage and also etymologically. "Conscious thinker," is most likely wrapped in quotes to highlight the fact that "conscious thinking" is different from our normal thinking.

Gurdjieff insists that there are two kinds of "mentation." He chooses the word "mentation" rather than "thinking" for a reason. "Mentation" is an act of the mind whereas "mentation by thought" is an act of the intellectual center, depending heavily on its use and manipulation of words. This he signals in the phrase: "mentation by thought, in which words, always possessing a relative sense, are employed."

> *The second kind of mentation, that is, "mentation by form," by which, strictly speaking, the exact sense of all writing must be also perceived, and after conscious confrontation with information already possessed, be assimilated,...*

form: c. 1200, *forme, fourme,* "semblance, image, likeness," from Old French *forme, fourme,* "physical form, appearance; pleasing looks; shape, image; way, manner" (12c.), from Latin *forma* "form, contour, figure, shape; appearance, looks; an outline, a model, pattern, design; sort, kind condition," a word of unknown prior origin. From c. 1300 as "physical shape (of something), contour, outline," of a person, "shape of the body;" also "appearance, likeness;" also "the imprint of an object." From c. 1300 as "correct or appropriate way of doing something; established procedure; traditional usage; formal etiquette." Mid-14c. as "instrument for shaping; a mould;" late 14c. as "way in which something is done," also "pattern of a manufactured object." Used widely from late 14c. in theology and Platonic philosophy with senses "archetype of a thing or class; Platonic essence of a thing; the formative principle."

The text is a suggestion to the reader that they consider their personal "mentation by form." The word "form" indicates a mode of thinking based on images, not words. The implication is that, in "mentation by form," an image is invoked in association with a word or collection of words, through sensation. He writes:

> *Accordingly, in the brains of people of different races and conditions dwelling in different geographical localities, there are formed about one and the same thing or even idea, a number of quite independent forms, which during functioning, that is to say, association, evoke in their being some sensation or other which subjectively conditions a definite picturing, and which picturing is expressed by this, that, or the other word, that serves only for its outer subjective expression.*

> *That is why each word, for the same thing or idea, almost always acquires for people of different geographical locality and race a very definite and entirely different so to say "inner content."*

In other words, if we consider a simple word like "house," any image that might arise in association with that word would be different for someone from Paris compared to someone from New York, and different again for someone who lived in rural France or rural America. The subjective associations to it would be different, arising from the experience of the house, which would vary by culture, and would include personal experience.

Clearly the difference in meaning of conceptual words, such as "justice" or "intelligence," would be equally tainted by the personal and cultural context within which they were experienced and the associations that were formed.

Gurdjieff asserts in the text that "mentation by form" is proper to all animals as well as to man. This implies that "mentation by form" is a function of the emotional center and moving/instinctive centers. As only man has an intellectual center, "mentation by thought" is possible for man alone.

For clarity consider these examples:

- "The letter 'u' is a vowel." The meaning here is only amenable to "mentation by thought." Different people have no difficulty agreeing about this.

- "It is going to rain." The experienced meaning of this may vary according to location. If in a hot climate then the words may convey a feeling of relief. If in a cold climate then perhaps a feeling of disappointment. The meaning may vary even person to person.

Gurdjieff says that, strictly speaking, the exact sense of all writing must also be perceived using "mentation by form," so that, when reading his words, we must also perceive their sense through the forms or images they evoke. When we read about red chillies and red skies, the word "red" has a different meaning. He says more about how our perception might work, when he says that:

> the exact sense of all writing must be also perceived, and after conscious confrontation with information already possessed, be assimilated,...

The reader will likely gloss over these words, but note that he suggests readers should "consciously confront" the meaning of what they read before assimilating (or digesting) it.

confrontation: 1630s, "action of bringing two parties face to face," for examination and discovery of the truth, from Medieval Latin *confrontationem* (nominative *confrontatio*), noun of action from

154

past-participle stem of *confrontari,* from assimilated form of Latin *com* "with, together" + *frontem* (nominative *frons*) "forehead."

assimilate: early 15c., in physiology, "absorb into and make part of the body," from Latin *assimilatus,* past participle of *assimilare, assimulare* "to make like, copy, imitate, assume the form of; feign, pretend," from assimilated form of *ad* "to" + *simulare* "make similar," from *similis* "like, resembling, of the same kind." Meaning "make alike, cause to resemble," and intransitive sense "become incorporated into" are from 1620s. In linguistics, "bring into accordance or agreement in speech," from 1854.

He talks about the consequences of the differences in the development of "mentation by form" in people with different upbringings, throwing more light on the process of mentation.

> *Accordingly, in the brains of people of different races and conditions dwelling in different geographical localities, there are formed about one and the same thing or even idea, a number of quite independent forms, which during functioning, that is to say, association, evoke in their being some sensation or other which subjectively conditions a definite picturing, and which is expressed by this, that, or the other word, that serves only for its outer subjective expression.*

Here he describes a chain of links from a thing or idea to a form, which evokes a sensation, conditioning a picturing, which is expressed by a word.

evoke: 1620s, from French *évoquer* or directly from Latin *evocare* "call out, rouse, summon," from assimilated form of *ex* "out" + *vocare* "to call." Often more or less with a sense of "calling spirits," or being called by them. Of feelings, memories, etc., by 1856.

condition: late 15c., "to make conditions, stipulate," from condition (n.). Meaning "subject to something as a condition" is from 1520s; sense of "form a prerequisite of" is from 1868. Meaning "to bring to a desired condition" is from 1844; psychological sense of "teach or accustom (a person or animal) to certain habits or responses" is from 1909.

Gurdjieff restates the problem surrounding the objective understanding of words.

> *In other words, if in the entirety of any man who has arisen and been formed in any locality, from the results of the specific local influences and impressions a certain "form" has been composed, and this form evokes in him by association the sensation of a definite "inner content," and consequently of a definite picturing or notion for the expression of*

which he employs one or another word which has eventually become habitual, and as I have said, subjective to him, then the hearer of that word, in whose being, owing to different conditions of his arising and growth, there has been formed concerning the given word a form of a different "inner content," will always perceive and of course infallibly understand that same word in quite another sense.

Gurdjieff warns us again that he will not write as "professional writers" usually write, and advises us to reflect seriously before reading any further.

If not, I am afraid for your hearing and other perceptive and also digestive organs which may be already so thoroughly automatized to the "literary language of the intelligentsia" existing in the present period of time on Earth, that the reading of these writings of mine might affect you very, very cacophonously, and from this you might lose your . . . you know what? . . . your appetite for your favorite dish and for your psychic specificness which particularly titillates your "inside" and which proceeds in you on seeing your neighbor, the brunette.

Gurdjieff uses the pacing of the words "you might lose your . . . you know what? . . ." to focus our attention on our physical and amorous appetites, and how the cacophonous effect of his writing might cause us to lose them.

cacophony: (n.) 1650s, "harsh or unpleasant sound," probably via French *cacophonie* (16c.), from a Latinized form of Greek *kakophonia*, from *kakophonos* "harsh sounding," from *kakos* "bad, evil." Meaning "discordant sounds in music" is from 1789.

For such a possibility, ensuing from my language, or rather, strictly speaking, from the form of my mentation, I am, thanks to oft-repeated past experiences, already quite as convinced with my whole being as a "thoroughbred donkey" is convinced of the right and justice of his obstinacy.

donkey: familiar term for an ass, 1785, also *donky, donkie*, originally slang or dialectal, of uncertain origin. Perhaps a diminutive from *dun* "dull gray-brown." Donkeys are notoriously stubborn, so the word was applied to stupid, obstinate, or wrong-headed persons by 1840.

thoroughbred: The earliest meaning, 1701, applied to persons, "thoroughly accomplished," from thorough + past tense of breed. In reference to horses, "of pure breed or stock," from 1796; the noun is first recorded 1842.

Now that I have warned you of what is most important, I am already tranquil about everything further. Even if any misunderstanding should arise on account of my writings, you alone will be entirely to blame, and my conscience will be as clear as for instance . . . the ex-Kaiser Wilhelm's.

Ex-Kaiser Wilhelm was the last German Emperor (Kaiser) and King of Prussia. He assumed the throne in 1888, launching Germany on a warlike course, resulting in the outbreak of World War I, when he gave German backing to Austria-Hungary against Serbia, following the assassination of Archduke Ferdinand of Austria. After Germany's defeat in 1918, Wilhelm lost the support of the German army, abdicated and fled to exile in the Netherlands, where he died in 1941.

Gurdjieff is probably being ironic here, as he knows almost all readers will ignore his warning.

After this passage, Gurdjieff goes on to talk about his motive for writing:

In all probability you are now thinking that I am, of course, a young man with an auspicious exterior and, as some express it, a "suspicious interior," and that, as a novice in writing, I am evidently intentionally being eccentric in the hope of becoming famous and thereby rich.

auspicious: 1590s, "of good omen" (implied in *auspiciously*), from Latin *auspicium* "divination by observing the flight of birds," from auspex (genitive *auspicis*) + -ous.

suspicious: (adj.) mid-14c., "deserving of or exciting suspicion," from Old French *sospecious*, from Latin *suspiciosus, suspitiosus* "exciting suspicion, causing mistrust," also "full of suspicion, ready to suspect," from stem of *suspicere* "look up at." Meaning "full of suspicion, inclined to suspect" in English is attested from c. 1400.

First of all, I am not young; I have already lived so much that I have been in my life, as it is said, "not only through the mill but through all the grindstones"; and secondly, I am in general not writing so as to make a career for myself, or so as to plant myself, as is said, "firmfootedly," thanks to this profession, which, I must add, in my opinion provides many openings to become a candidate d-i-r-e-c-t for "Hell"—assuming of course that such people can in general by their Being, perfect themselves even to that extent, for the reason that knowing nothing whatsoever themselves, they write all kinds of "claptrap" and thereby automatically acquiring authority, they become

157

almost one of the chief factors, the totality of which steadily continues year by year, still further to diminish the, without this, already extremely diminished psyche of people.

We know that Gurdjieff was "not young" when *The Tales* was published. The phrase "not only through the mill but through all the grindstones" may derive from 2nd century Greek philosopher Sextus Empiricus, who wrote "The millstones of the gods grind late, but they grind fine."

claptrap: 1730, "a trick to 'catch' applause," a stage term; from clap + trap (n.). Extended sense of "cheap, showy language" is from 1819; hence "nonsense, rubbish."

And as regards my personal career, then thanks to all forces high and low and, if you like, even right and left, I have actualized it long ago, and have already long been standing on "firm feet" and even maybe on very good feet, and I moreover am certain that their strength is sufficient for many more years, in spite of all my past, present, and future enemies.

He uses the term "firm-footedly" earlier and "firm feet" in this paragraph. It could be taken to mean "firm or secure financial position," although the intended meaning may go deeper. Gurdjieff uses directions here – high, low, left and right, reminiscent perhaps of the Christian ritual of making the sign of the cross. We may also wonder if the use of "firm feet" in this context might relate to Christianity, since it is wrapped in quotes. If so, then it may relate to this New Testament passage (International Standard Version), Epheians 6:15.

and being firm-footed in the gospel of peace

Also, there is the prayer mentioned in the Chapter on The Holy Planet "Purgatory" as a formulation of the Law of Three:

'Holy God,
Holy Firm,
Holy Immortal,
Have mercy on us'

The final paragraph of this section describes Gurdjieff's idea of allowing readers to return the book after reading the warnings in *The Arousing of Thought*.

Yes, I think you might as well be told also about an idea which has only just arisen in my madcap brain, and namely, specially to request the printer, to whom I shall give my first book, to print this first chapter

*of my writings in such a way that anybody may read it before cutting
the pages of the book itself, whereupon, on learning that it is not written
in the usual manner, that is to say, for helping to produce in one's
mentation, very smoothly and easily, exciting images and lulling
reveries, he may, if he wishes, without wasting words with the
bookseller, return it and get his money back, money perhaps earned by
the sweat of his own brow.*

In Gurdjieff's time, some books were sold with their pages "uncut." The term
"uncut" is used to describe a book with the pages still attached to the adjacent
page at the top or fore edge. With such a book, the reader cuts the pages with
a paper knife in order to read the book.

> **madcap:** 1580s, noun ("person who acts madly or wildly") and adjective
> ("wild, harum-scarum"), from mad + cap, used figuratively for "head." The
> "cap" part is an old (obsolete in any other use) word meaning "head." So a
> "madcap" was originally a "mad-head," someone who "has bats in their
> belfry."

> **lull:** (v.) early 14c., *lullen* "to calm or hush to sleep," probably imitative
> of *lu-lu* sound used to lull a child to sleep (compare Swedish *lulla* "to hum
> a lullaby," German *lullen* "to rock," Middle Dutch *lollen* "to mutter").
> Figurative use from 1570s; specifically "to quiet (suspicion) so as to delude
> into a sense of security" is from c. 1600.

> **reverie:** (n.) mid-14c., *reuerye*, "wild conduct, frolic," from Old
> French *reverie*, *resverie* "revelry, raving, delirium" (Modern French *rêverie*),
> from *resver* "to dream, wander, rave" (12c., Modern French *rêver*), of uncertain
> origin. Meaning "daydream" is first attested 1650s, a reborrowing from French.
> As a type of musical composition, it is attested from 1880.

He emphasizes again that the book "is not written in the usual manner, for
helping to produce in one's mentation, very smoothly and easily, exciting
images and lulling reveries."

The 1931 Manuscript

The reference to hobbies and some of the associated text is not present in *The
1931 Manuscript*, and some of the details of the perception and assimilation of
the exact sense of all writing is also missing. The wording thereafter is similar,
although the mention of "your neighbor, the brunette" is missing.

There is a significant difference between *The 1931 Manuscript* and *The Tale*s on
the subject of arranging for the printer and booksellers to allow potential

readers to return the book after having been put off by the warnings. In *The 1931 Manuscript* there is an extensive extra passage, repeated below, explaining that Gurdjieff wishes to assign a definite sum of money for the misunderstandings which may arise when the uncut books are returned to the bookseller.

> *While writing and cogitating how to explain this idea to Mr. Printer, there arose unsought in this madcap brain of mine, another idea quite disadvantageous for me personally, namely, the idea to be sure to assign a definite sum of money for the misunderstandings which may arise when the uncut books are returned to the bookseller.*
>
> *The disadvantage to myself in this idea which has spontaneously arisen in my madcap brain consists chiefly in this; that I shall be forced to take this money from a fund, dependent solely on my own will, free from the advice or disagreement of others, misbegotten busybodies, always around me, and, namely, from what is called my "Crayfish-fund."*
>
> *Now that I happen to be speaking of this fund of mine, which depends solely on my independent will, objective justice demands that I should not fail, first of all, to praise and extol with an impulse of great affection and sentiment the names of the noble "Uncle Sam" and "John Bull," and then, with an impulse of gratitude, to remark that during several years, genuine sprigs of those names I have just extolled, who for various objective merits have become worthy to rank as "Crayfish-idiots," have hitherto always punctually and even with unction kept supplied and so far still supply this solitary hearth of my, so to say, hopes and expectations.*

Gurdjieff says he will need to use his "Crayfish fund," which he alone controls, in order to fund his idea about selling his book partly uncut. Gurdjieff used the word "crayfish" to describe the funding parties he held, as described in *The Gurdjieff Years 1929-1949* by Louise Goepfert March:

> *On Sunday evenings Gurdjieff and his "tail" (the entourage of students, family, and guests who followed him everywhere) always went to a restaurant in Montmartre. These meals were referred to as "Crayfish Parties" because of the small shrimp-like crustaceans served in abundance. My task was to find someone to cover the bill. If I couldn't get one of the guests at the Prieure to pay, I had, as I often did, to ask "poor Miss Gordon" to provide the funds.*

He may be using the word "crayfish" symbolically. Crayfish are bottom-feeders. His "crayfish fund" could be thought of as the funds he gathered to support his work. The "crayfish idiots" are most likely those who attended his his dinners, including his funding dinners, where the ritual toasting of "the idiots" took place.

> *It must be allowed that by reducing the number of my so to say "crayfish-parasites," who have become indispensable assistants in what has lately become, as it were, a necessity for my recreation, I ought to be able also to provide that sum of money from this fund, but owing to that specific and moreover terrible disease, always chronic and, lately, on the increase among the poor and wretched money-changers, which disease has become well known on the Earth under the description of being "hell-bent," not even such a self-deprivation can save me, because on account of this terrible disease, it has already now become extremely difficult for me to make both ends meet.*

The crayfish-parasites may be a reference to those of his pupils whom he supported at the Prieuré, and many of whom he later sent away.

recreation: late 14c., "refreshment or curing of a person, refreshment by eating," from Old French *recreacion* (13c.), from Latin *recreationem* (nominative *recreatio*) "recovery from illness," noun of action from past participle stem of *recreare* "to refresh, restore, make anew, revive, invigorate," from re- "again" (see re-) + *creare* "create." Meaning "refresh oneself by some amusement" is first recorded c. 1400.

> *Eh . . . Ekh! . . . unfortunate me, hapless victim of a combination of planetary influences at the moment of my appearance here below!*
>
> *This time also it is already beyond doubt—as it has happened to me many a time before my arrival in Europe—that on account of this altruistic intention which spontaneously arose in me, all the rest of the parts of my entire whole will once again "totally-unexpectedly" be made the "scapegoats."*
>
> *It has always been so; no sooner does an idea arise in my madcap brain, but it inexorably compels the whole of me to carry it out at any cost, as for instance in the present case, to assign without fail the said sum of money, when, in fact, I have none, nor are there in sight any likely "fat-sheep-for-shearing."*

This whole passage seems to indicate the onset of the great depression which impacted him as much as anyone else in that era. Most likely the reason he removed this passage from *The Tales* was that, as time passed, it ceased to be relevant.

9

The Transcaucasian Kurd

"You must see that in life, you receive exactly what you give, life is the mirror of what you are; it is in your own likeness."

~ Gurdjieff

—◊—

I shall do this without fail, moreover, because I just now again remember the story of what happened to a Transcaucasian Kurd, which story I heard in my quite early youth and which in subsequent years, whenever I recalled it in corresponding cases, engendered in me an enduring and inextinguishable impulse of tenderness. I think it will be very useful for me, and also for you, if I relate this story to you somewhat in detail.

It will be useful chiefly because I have decided already to make the "salt," or as contemporary pureblooded Jewish businessmen would say, the "Tzimus" of this story, one of the basic principles of that new literary form which I intend to employ for the attainment of the aim I am now pursuing by means of this new profession of mine.

This Transcaucasian Kurd once set out from his village on some business or other to town, and there in the market he saw in a fruiterer's shop a handsomely arranged display of all kinds of fruit.

In this display, he noticed one "fruit," very beautiful in both color and form, and its appearance so took his fancy and he so longed to try it, that in spite of his having scarcely any money, he decided to buy without fail at least one of these gifts of Great Nature, and taste it.

Then, with intense eagerness, and with a courage not customary to him, he entered the shop and pointing with his horny finger to the "fruit" which had taken his fancy he asked the shopkeeper its price. The shopkeeper replied that a pound of the "fruit" would cost two cents.

Finding that the price was not at all high for what in his opinion was such a beautiful fruit, our Kurd decided to buy a whole pound.

Having finished his business in town, he set off again on foot for home the same day.

Walking at sunset over the hills and dales, and willynilly perceiving the exterior visibility of those enchanting parts of the bosom of Great Nature, the Common Mother, and involuntarily inhaling a pure air uncontaminated by the usual exhalations of industrial towns, our Kurd quite naturally suddenly felt a wish to gratify himself with some ordinary food also; so sitting down by the side of the road, he took from his provision bag some bread and the "fruit" he had bought which had looked so good to him, and leisurely began to eat.

But . . . horror of horrors! . . . very soon everything inside him began to burn. But in spite of this he kept on eating.

And this hapless biped creature of our planet kept on eating, thanks only

To fret about it now and to think up some measure less detrimental for me, it is already too late. So it pleases Fate. But meanwhile, I think it will not be useless and may perhaps be productive for me as well as instructive for you, if I relate to you somewhat in detail the story of what happened to the mentioned Transcaucasian Kurd.

And it may be productive for me and instructive for you because I have already categorically decided to make use in my proposed writings of the very "Tzimus" of this story also for the actualization of the aims I have in view.

This Transcaucasian Kurd once set out from his village on some business or other to town, and there in the market he saw in a fruiterer's shop, a handsomely arranged display of all kinds of fruit.

In this display he noticed one fruit, very beautiful in both color and form, and its appearance so took his fancy and he so longed to try it, that, in spite of his having scarcely any money, he decided that he couldn't not buy at least just one of these fruits, and try it.

With intense eagerness and with an audacity not common to him, he entered the shop and pointing with his horny finger at the fruit which had taken his fancy, he asked the shopkeeper its price.

The shopkeeper replied that a pound of the fruit would cost "six-groschen."

Finding that this price was not at all high, our Kurd decided to buy a whole pound.

Having finished his business in town, he set off for home the same day. Walking at sunset over the hills and dales, and perceiving the exterior visibility of those enchanting scenes of the bosom of Great Nature, the common mother, and there inhaling a pure air uncontaminated by the usual exhalations of industrial towns, our Kurd quite naturally suddenly felt a wish to gratify himself with some ordinary food also; so sitting down by the side of the road he took from his provision-bag some bread and fruit he had brought that had looked so good to him and began to eat.

But . . . oh horror! . . . very soon, everything inside him began to burn.

But in spite of this he kept on eating. And this hapless biped creature of to that particular human inherency which I mentioned at first, the principle of which I intended, when I decided to use it as the foundation of the new literary form I have created, to make, as it were, a "guiding beacon" leading me to one of my aims in view, and the sense and meaning of which moreover you will, I am sure, soon grasp—of course according to the degree of your comprehension—during the reading of any subsequent chapter of my writings, if, of course, you take the risk and read further, or, it may perhaps be that even at the end of this first chapter you will already "smell" something.

And so, just at the moment when our Kurd was overwhelmed by all the unusual sensations proceeding within him from this strange repast on the bosom of Nature, there came along the same road a fellow villager of his, one reputed by those who knew him to be very clever and experienced; and, seeing that the whole face of the Kurd was aflame, that his eyes were streaming with tears, and that in spite of this, as if intent upon the fulfillment of his most important duty, he was eating real "red pepper pods," he said to him:

"What are you doing, you Jericho jackass? You'll be burnt alive! Stop eating that extraordinary product, so unaccustomed for your nature."

But our Kurd replied: "No, for nothing on Earth will I stop. Didn't I pay my last two cents for them? Even if my soul departs from my body I shall still go on eating."

Whereupon our resolute Kurd—it must of course be assumed that he was such—did not stop, but continued eating the "red pepper pods."

After what you have just perceived, I hope there may already be arising in your mentation a corresponding mental association which should, as a result, effectuate in you, as it sometimes happens to contemporary people, that which you call, in general, understanding, and that in the present case you will understand just why I, well knowing and having many a time our planet kept on eating only thanks to that same particular human inherency which I first mentioned, and which was just what I had in view when I began to relate the present story, and the sense and meaning of which moreover you will, I am sure soon grasp—of course, according to the degree of your resourcefulness—during the reading of any subsequent chapter of my writings, assuming, of course, that you take the risk and read further, or, it may perhaps be that you will even already "smell" something at the end of this warning of mine.

Meanwhile I boldly or, if you like, impudently, take it upon myself in advance to advise you to absorb with, as might be said, an "intensive-mobilization" of all your perceptive organs, the information elaborating the rest of this story, in order that the crystallization in you of the new impression may proceed normally and not in the manner in which it has already become habitual for this to proceed, that is to say, as the great sage Mullah Nassr Eddin defines and expresses it: "One part is used up for one's own welfare, and that only for today, while all the rest going in at one ear, is exhausted in the process of trying to get out at the other."

Well then, just at the moment when our Kurd was overwhelmed by all the unusual sensations proceeding within him from this strange repast on the bosom of Nature, there came along the same road a fellow-villager of his, once reputed by those who knew him to be very clever and experienced; and seeing that the whole face of our Kurd was aflame, that his eyes were streaming with tears, and that in spite of this, as if intent upon the fulfilment of his most important duty, he was eating real "red-pepper-pods," he said to him:

"What are you doing, you jackass! You'll be burnt alive! Stop eating that extraordinary and, for your nature, unaccustomed product."

But our Kurd replied:

"No, not for anything on Earth will I stop. Didn't I pay my last 'six-groschen' for them? Even if my soul leaves my body, I shall go on eating."

Whereupon our resolute Kurd—it must, of course, be assumed that he was such—did not stop, but continued eating the "red-pepper-pods."

After what you have just perceived, esteemed buyer of my writings, I hope—of course only faintly—that there may already be arising in your mentation a corresponding association which should, as a result, bring about as it happens sometimes to some people, what you call an understanding, and that in the present case you will understand just why I, commiserated with this human inherency, the inevitable manifestation of which is that if anybody pays money for something, he is bound to use it to the end, was animated in the whole of my entirety with the idea, arisen in my mentation, to take every possible measure in order that you, as is said "my brother in appetite and in spirit"—in the event of your proving to be already accustomed to reading books, though of all kinds, yet nevertheless only those written exclusively in the aforesaid "language of the intelligentsia"—having already paid money for my writings and learning only afterwards that they are not written in the usual convenient and easily read language, should not be compelled as a consequence of the said human inherency, to read my writings through to the end at all costs, as our poor Transcaucasian Kurd was compelled to go on with his eating of what he had fancied for its appearance alone—that "not to be joked with" noble red pepper.

And so, for the purpose of avoiding any misunderstanding through this inherency, the data for which are formed in the entirety of contemporary man, thanks evidently to his frequenting of the cinema and thanks also to his never missing an opportunity of looking into the left eye of the other sex, I wish that this commencing chapter of mine should be printed in the said manner, so that everyone can read it through without cutting the pages of the book itself.

Otherwise the bookseller will, as is said, "cavil," and will without fail again turn out to act in accordance with the basic principle of booksellers in general, formulated by them in the words: "You'll be more of a simpleton than a fisherman if you let go of the fish which has swallowed the bait," and will decline to take back a book whose pages you have cut. I have no doubt of this possibility; indeed, I fully expect such lack of conscience on the part of the booksellers.

And the data for the engendering of my certainty as to this lack of conscience on the part of these booksellers were completely formed in me, when, while I was a professional "Indian Fakir," I needed, for the complete elucidation of a certain "ultra-philosophical" question also to become familiar, among other things, with the associative process for the manifestation of the automatically constructed psyche of contemporary booksellers and of their salesmen when palming off books on their buyers.

Knowing all this and having become, since the misfortune which befell well knowing and having many a time commiserated with this human inherency—whose inevitable manifestation takes the form that if anybody pays money for something he is bound to use it to the end—was seized with the idea, to take every possible measure in order that you, my "neighbor"—in the event that you should prove to be already accustomed to reading books, though of any kind yet nevertheless only those written exclusively in the mentioned "language-of-the-intelligentsia"—having already paid money for my writings and learning only afterwards that they are not written in the usual easily and comfortably read language, should not be compelled, as a consequence of the said human inherency, to read my writings through to the end at all costs, as our poor Transcaucasian Kurd was compelled to continue eating what he had taken a fancy to from its appearance alone—that "not-to- be-joked-with" noble "red-pepper."

For the purpose of avoiding any misunderstanding through this inherency in man, I wish that this warning of mine may be printed in the said manner, so that everyone can read it through without cutting the pages of the book itself.

Otherwise I am very much afraid that the bookseller may, in that case also, try to make a profit for himself and decline to take back a book whose pages had once been cut.

I have no doubt of this possibility, and I fully expect such unconscionableness on their part.

And the data for the engendering of my certainty as to their unconscionableness were acquired in me just when, while I was a professional "Indian-fakir," I happened to become familiar also with, among other things the various aspects of the psyche of contemporary booksellers and particularly with that of their clerks when palming off books on their buyers, and now, having become, since the misfortune which befell me, by nature just, in the maximum degree, I cannot help repeating, that is to say, I cannot help again warning you and even imploringly advising you before beginning to cut the pages of my first book,

The Tales

me, habitually just and fastidious in the extreme, I cannot help repeating, or rather, I cannot help again warning you, and even imploringly advising you, before beginning to cut the pages of this first book of mine, to read through very attentively, and even more than once, this first chapter of my writings.

But in the event that notwithstanding this warning of mine, you should, nevertheless, wish to become acquainted with the further contents of my expositions, then there is already nothing else left for me to do but to wish you with all my "genuine soul" a very, very good appetite, and that you may "digest" all that you read, not only for your own health but for the health of all those near you.

I said "with my genuine soul" because recently living in Europe and coming in frequent contact with people who on every appropriate and inappropriate occasion are fond of taking in vain every sacred name which should belong only to man's inner life, that is to say, with people who swear to no purpose, I being, as I have already confessed, a follower in general not only of the theoretical— as contemporary people have become—but also of the practical sayings of popular wisdom which have become fixed by the centuries, and therefore of the saying which in the present case corresponds to what is expressed by the words: "When you are in Rome do as Rome does," decided, in order not to be out of harmony with the custom established here in Europe of swearing in ordinary conversation, and at the same time to act according to the commandment which was enunciated by the holy lips of Saint Moses "not to take the holy names in vain," to make use of one of those examples of the "newly baked" fashionable languages of the present time, namely English, and so from then on, I began on necessary occasions to swear by my "English soul."

The point is that in this fashionable language, the words "soul" and the bottom of your foot, also called "sole," are pronounced and even written almost alike.

I do not know how it is with you, who are already partly candidate for a buyer of my writings, but my peculiar nature cannot, even with a great mental desire, avoid being indignant at the fact manifested by people of contemporary civilization, that the very highest in man, particularly beloved by our COMMON FATHER CREATOR, can really be named, and indeed very often before even having made clear to oneself what it is, can be understood to be that which is lowest and dirtiest in man.

to read through very attentively and even more than once this Warning of mine.

But in case you decide and notwithstanding this Warning of mine, should wish to become acquainted with the further contents of my "wiseacrings," then there is already nothing else left for me to do but to wish you with all my genuine soul an excellent appetite, and that you may "digest" all that you may read not only for your own health, but also for the health of all those near to you.

I say with my "genuine-soul" because it is a habit of mine to refer often to what is called my "English-soul"; but why it is a habit of mine, I suggest that you puzzle out for yourself, assuming, of course, that there is or should arise in you any curiosity to learn how easily the very highest and most particularly beloved of our ALL-MAINTAINING CREATOR may unconsciously be taken for the very lowest in man.

Well, enough of "philologizing." Let us return to the main task of this initial chapter, destined, among other things, on the one hand to stir up the drowsy thoughts in me as well as in the reader, and, on the other, to warn the reader about something.

And so, I have already composed in my head the plan and sequence of the intended expositions, but what form they will take on paper, I, speaking frankly, myself do not as yet know with my consciousness, but with my subconsciousness I already definitely feel that on the whole it will take the form of something which will be, so to say, "hot," and will have an effect on the entirety of every reader such as the red pepper pods had on the poor Transcaucasian Kurd.

Now that you have become familiar with the story of our common countryman, the Transcaucasian Kurd, I already consider it my duty to make a confession and hence before continuing this first chapter, which is by way of an introduction to all my further predetermined writings, I wish to bring to the knowledge of what is called your "pure waking consciousness" the fact that in the writings following this chapter of warning I shall expound my thoughts intentionally in such sequence and with such "logical confrontation," that the essence of certain real notions may of themselves automatically, so to say, go from this "waking consciousness"—which most people in their ignorance mistake for the real consciousness, but which I affirm and experimentally prove is the fictitious one—into what you call the subconscious, which ought to be in my opinion the real human consciousness, and there by themselves mechanically bring about that transformation which should in general proceed in the entirety of a man and give him, from his own conscious mentation, the results he ought to have, which are proper to man and not merely to single- or double-brained animals.

I decided to do this without fail so that this initial chapter of mine, predetermined as I have already said to awaken your consciousness, should fully justify its purpose, and reaching not only your, in my opinion, as yet only fictitious "consciousness," but also your real consciousness, that is to say, what you call your subconscious, might, for the first time, compel you to reflect actively.

In the entirety of every man, irrespective of his heredity and education, there are formed two independent consciousnesses, which in their

The plan and sequence of my intended expositions I have already composed in my "swollen" head, but into what form they will mould themselves upon paper, I frankly confess that I myself do not know with my consciousness, though with the total result of the functioning of my instinct I already definitely feel that on the whole it will all mould itself into "something" so to say "hot," and will have an effect on the common presence of every reader like that which the "red-pepper-pods" had on the poor Transcaucasian Kurd.

functioning as well as in their manifestations have almost nothing in common. One consciousness is formed from the perception of all kinds of accidental, or on the part of others intentionally produced, mechanical impressions, among which must also be counted the "consonances" of various words which are indeed as is said empty; and the other consciousness is formed from the so to say, "already previously formed material results" transmitted to him by heredity, which have become blended with the corresponding parts of the entirety of a man, as well as from the data arising from his intentional evoking of the associative confrontations of these "materialized data" already in him.

The whole totality of the formation as well as the manifestation of this second human consciousness, which is none other than what is called the "subconscious," and which is formed from the "materialized results" of heredity and the confrontations actualized by one's own intentions, should in my opinion, formed by many years of my experimental elucidations during exceptionally favorably arranged conditions, predominate in the common presence of a man.

As a result of this conviction of mine which as yet doubtlessly seems to you the fruit of the fantasies of an afflicted mind, I cannot now, as you yourself see, disregard this second consciousness and, compelled by my essence, am obliged to construct the general exposition even of this first chapter of my writings, namely, the chapter which should be the preface for everything further, calculating that it should reach and, in the manner required for my aim, "ruffle" the perceptions accumulated in both these consciousnesses of yours. Continuing my expositions with this calculation, I must first of all inform your fictitious consciousness that, thanks to three definite peculiar data which were crystallized in my entirety during various periods of my preparatory age, I am really unique in respect of the so to say "muddling and befuddling" of all the notions and convictions supposedly firmly fixed in the entirety of people with whom I come in contact. Tut! Tut! Tut! . . . I already feel that in your "false"—but according to you "real"— consciousness, there are beginning to be agitated, like "blinded flies," all the chief data transmitted to you by heredity from your uncle and mother, the totality of which data, always and in everything, at least engenders in you the impulse—nevertheless extremely good—of curiosity, as in the given case, to find out as quickly as possible why I, that is to say, a novice at writing, whose name has not even once been mentioned in the newspapers,

The 1931 Manuscript

Thanks to the data crystallized in me which long ago became the main lever of my individuality, and about which I wish just now to inform you, I shall of course touch in my proposed writings upon questions not only of the everyday life of people, already so to say regularized on the Earth—an everyday life, it must be said, contracted—of course only in my opinion—to the point of wretchedness—but I shall also touch upon questions from which there must inevitably arise unusual sensations and uncommon picturings in all your separate relatively independent parts, which parts the ancient sages characterized as "falsely-ascribing-initiative-to-themselves"; namely, in your thoughts, your feelings, and simply in your body. The process of the beneficent Armagnac proceeding at the present moment in my common presence bids me confess to you and warn you that owing to the aforementioned data, the whole of my common presence, in the present period of my life, namely, just when from causes not dependent on me, I have now to become a professional writer, is already such that even with the whole of my mental categorical decision and desire, and with the help of all my separately spiritualized and independent parts—those educated of themselves as well as those educated intentionally by my own will, just that will of mine which flows from and is based exclusively only on my Pure Reason—which parts constitute in me as well as in you this common presence of mine—I cannot do otherwise than as the most exalted great terrestrial sage Mullah Nassr Eddin would say, "tangle-and-entangle" the whole of you, or as he also sometimes says, "put-you-in-galoshes," in full face of the fact that I am counting on your help, or rather on your money, which I shall receive thanks to your purchase of writings; for the full possibility of accomplishing even with a "flourish," my self-imposed and perhaps from your point of view, purely egoistic aim.

have suddenly become so unique. Never mind! I personally am very pleased with the arising of this curiosity even though only in your "false" consciousness, as I already know from experience that this impulse unworthy of man can sometimes even pass from this consciousness into one's nature and become a worthy impulse—the impulse of the desire for knowledge, which, in its turn, assists the better perception and even the closer understanding of the essence of any object on which, as it sometimes happens, the attention of a contemporary man might be concentrated, and therefore I am even willing, with pleasure, to satisfy this curiosity which has arisen in you at the present moment. Now listen and try to justify, and not to disappoint, my expectations. This original personality of mine, already "smelled out" by certain definite individuals from both choirs of the Judgment Seat Above, whence Objective justice proceeds, and also here on Earth, by as yet a very limited number of people, is based, as I already said, on three secondary specific data formed in me at different times during my preparatory age. The first of these data, from the very beginning of its arising, became as it were the chief directing lever of my entire wholeness, and the other two, the "vivifying-sources," as it were, for the feeding and perfecting of this first datum.

G urdjieff now proceeds to tell the story of the Transcaucasian Kurd, the memory of which appears to strengthen his resolve to print his book with the pages of the first chapter uncut, so that the reader may, if he so chooses, return the book to the book seller and get his money back.

Transcaucasia lies to south of the Caucasus Mountains, spanning the countries of Georgia, Azerbaijan and Armenia. To the north is Russia, to the east the Caspian Sea, and to the south Iran and Turkey. Kurdistan, the homeland of the Kurds, encircles Lake Van and the region south of Lake Urmia. Thus it spans a sizeable mountainous area south of Transcaucasia, which is primarily part of Turkey, but also northern Iraq and western Iran. The word *Transcaucasia* is a Latin rendering of the Russian-language word *Zakavkazie*, meaning (from the Russian perspective) "the area beyond the Caucasus Mountains." Historically, some Kurds have made their home in Transcaucasia. According to the 2011 Armenian Census, 37,470 Kurds currently live in Armenia.

Nowadays, the word "Caucasian" is frequently used to denote 'white, or of European origin,' especially in America. It is possible then that Gurdjieff is

The 1931 Manuscript

And now, my dear, as yet only candidate for my, so to say, future "voluntary-slaves," listen attentively and try your hardest without letting any thing escape you, to transubstantiate in your common presence the information concerning the arising of the original cause and also of those two events whose effects on the whole of me, having become by the Will of Fate, as contemporary scientists and pious pastors would say, "vivifying," served as factors for the accomplished crystallization in my common presence, of just those specific data on account of which, it may be said, firstly, that I am now an "exceptional-monster" among the many millions of animals similar to me, and secondly, that since in the present period of my existence I must become a professional writer, I am compelled to employ this new profession of mine, at whatever cost, as our esteemed Mullah Nassr Eddin has expressed it, to "tangle-and-entangle" all your, as you call them, "images" and "notions" you have until now acquired, which though they are your own attainments, are nevertheless, even in your frank opinion, "very-suspicious."

using the word Transcaucasian, not to denote inhabitants of the geographical area, but as a metaphor for Europeans and Americans.

If so, it may help to consider why Gurdjieff chose the word "Kurd." The word derives from the Sumerian word, *karda*, which means "mountain." This seems logical because the Kurds' homeland is mountainous. The Kurds were nomadic, and some are known to practice Sufism.

Elsewhere in his writings, Gurdjieff uses the term mountain (as does the New Testament) to indicate higher levels. So mountain dwellers can be thought of as those attracted to the higher, i.e. those who may be attracted to the Work.

All of which indicates that Transcaucasian Kurd suggests Europeans and Americans attracted to spiritual pursuits.

This may explain Gurdjieff's statement:

> *...in subsequent years, whenever I recalled it in corresponding cases, engendered in me an enduring and inextinguishable impulse of tenderness.*

Tzimus and Salt

Gurdjieff seems to indicate that the words "Tzimus" and "salt" have very similar meanings. This has created some confusion, because the origin of the word "Tzimus" is unclear. *Tsimes* (sometimes spelled *tsimmes* or *tzimmes*), which sounds plausibly similar, is a Yiddish word for an Ashkenazi (German /East European Jewish) stewed dish made variously of carrots, prunes and sometimes meat. It is not salty, but sweet, and for that reason it is particularly associated with Rosh Hashanah (New Year). A Yiddish expert suggested that *tsimes* also means "mess," "disorder," or "fuss" and may be Slavonic in origin. It is probably not the origin of "Tzimus."

Most likely, Gurdjieff borrowed "Tzimus" from Russian. Marvin Grossman, in an article in the *Gurdjieff International Review*, dealt with it at length, concluding that it is Russian slang, means pith or essence, and is a word favored by Russian Jews.

This makes sense in that "pith" and "salt" are at least similar in meaning.

Without salt, food can lack flavor, so it is a valuable commodity, particularly if it is difficult to obtain. The Romans used it as a salary, in the sense that "salt-money" was a Roman soldier's allowance for the purchase of salt. It is one of the basic elements of life.

"Salt" is possibly a Christian reference, from the sermon on the mount, as follows:

> Ye are the salt of the earth: but if the salt have lost his savour, wherewith shall it be salted? it is thenceforth good for nothing, but to be cast out, and to be trodden under foot of men. Ye are the light of the world. A city that is set on an hill cannot be hid. [Matt.5 Verses 13 to 20, King James version.]

According to Brian Simmons in *The Passion Translation New Testament (2nd Edition)*: "Rabbinical literature equates salt with wisdom." Also salt is a preservative and in alchemy it symbolizes 'that which survives the fire.'

Gurdjieff writes:

> It will be useful chiefly because I have decided already to make the "salt," or as contemporary pureblooded Jewish businessmen would say, the "Tzimus" of this story, one of the basic principles of that new literary form which I intend to employ for the attainment of the aim I am now pursuing by means of this new profession of mine.

The reference to "contemporary pureblooded Jewish businessmen" may be to give a context to the word "Tzimus," to enable the reader to track the origin of the word. In any case, both "Tzimus" and "salt" are wrapped in quotes, suggesting the reader pay particular attention.

The use of the word "pureblooded" is curious, and most likely metaphorical. The Jews are a people with a culture and a religion which admits "outbreeding," although it was relatively uncommon.

Gurdjieff indicates that the story of the Transcaucasian Kurd uses "one of the basic principles of that new literary form which I intend to employ."

This may mean that Gurdjieff is using a multitude of metaphors to relay meaning. As we shall see, the story of the Transcaucasian Kurd can be viewed in that way.

The Transcaucasian Kurd

On the surface, the story implies that the Kurd is a naive individual from the country. He buys some fruit that he has never seen nor tried before and discovers that it burns the mouth and is not palatable at all. However, it can be read in a different way.

> This Transcaucasian Kurd once set out from his village on some business or other to town, and there in the market he saw in a fruiterer's shop a handsomely arranged display of all kinds of fruit.

There is a definite contrast in the text between a village and a town. Historically and etymologically, the word village (late 14c.) meant "inhabited place larger than a hamlet, but smaller than a town." By contrast, the word "town" indicates a large settlement, possibly fortified. Towns usually have markets whereas villages do not.

Later Gurdjieff refers to the Kurd as "our common countryman". We appreciate this later in the chapter on Atlantis. The member of Beelzebub's tribe that makes the wager with King Appolis in Atlantis is referred to throughout as a countryman. The etymology of country shows the same derivation as the word counter. It referred originally to something opposite something else, and the country was always opposite the town.

market: early 12c., "a meeting at a fixed time for buying and selling livestock and provisions, an occasion on which goods are publicly exposed for sale and buyers assemble to purchase," from Old North French market "marketplace, trade, commerce" (Old French marchiet, Modern French marché), from Latin mercatus "trading, buying and

179

selling; trade; market" (source of Italian *mercato*, Spanish mercado, Dutch *markt*, German *Markt*), from past participle of *mercari* "to trade, deal in, buy," from *merx* (genitive *mercis*) "wares, merchandise." This is from an Italic root *merk-*, possibly from Etruscan, referring to various aspects of economics.

business: Old English *bisignes* (Northumbrian) "care, anxiety, occupation," from *bisig* "careful, anxious, busy, occupied, diligent" (see busy (adj.)) + -ness. The original sense is obsolete, as is the Middle English sense of "state of being much occupied or engaged" (mid-14c.), the latter replaced by busyness. Johnson's dictionary also has busiless "at leisure; without business; unemployed." Modern two-syllable pronunciation is 17c. Sense of "a person's work, occupation, that which one does for a livelihood" is first recorded late 14c. (in late Old English *bisig* (adj.) appears as a noun with the sense "occupation, state of employment"). Sense of "that which is undertaken as a duty" is from late 14c. Meaning "what one is about at the moment" is from 1590s. Sense of "trade, commercial engagements, mercantile pursuits collectively" is first attested 1727, on the notion of "matters which occupy one's time and attention." In 17c. business also could mean "sexual intercourse."

In this display, he noticed one "fruit," very beautiful in both color and form, and its appearance so took his fancy and he so longed to try it, that in spite of his having scarcely any money, he decided to buy without fail at least one of these gifts of Great Nature, and taste it.

Fruit

We note that "fruit" is wrapped in quotes.

fruit: late 12c., "any vegetable product useful to humans or animals," from Old French *fruit* "fruit, fruit eaten as dessert; harvest; virtuous action" (12c.), from Latin *fructus* "an enjoyment, delight, satisfaction; proceeds, produce, fruit, crops," from frug-, stem of *frui* "to use, enjoy," from suffixed form of PIE root *bhrug-* "to enjoy," with derivatives referring to agricultural products. The Latin word also is the source of Spanish *fruto*, Italian *frutto*, German *Frucht*, Swedish *frukt-*. Originally in English meaning all products of the soil (vegetables, nuts, grain, acorns); modern narrower sense is from early 13c. Also "income from agricultural produce, revenue or profits from the soil" (mid-14c.), hence, "profit," the classical sense preserved in fruits of (one's) labor. Meaning "offspring, progeny, child" is from mid-13c.; that of "any consequence, outcome, or result" is from late 14c. Meaning "odd person, eccentric" is from 1910; that of "male homosexual" is from 1935, underworld slang. The term also is noted in 1931 as tramp slang for "a girl or woman willing to oblige," probably from the fact of being "easy picking." Fruit salad recorded from 1861; fruit-cocktail from 1900; fruit-bat by 1869.

Symbolically, fruit is the produce of man (New Testament: "by their fruit ye shall know them"). So possibly this is the produce of real man. And in the context of *The Tales* we would be inclined to believe that.

Gurdjieff uses the symbols of "town" and "market" on the one hand and "countryside" on the other to represent personality and essence, both here and elsewhere in *The Tales*. The town represents life in the fourth way sense of the place to apply the Work. So the Kurd, who is primarily of essence (the countryside), goes into town and into the market and sees a fruit that he would only encounter in a town and is attracted to it.

fancy: mid-15c., fantsy "inclination, liking," contraction of fantasy. It took the older and longer word's sense of "inclination, whim, desire." Meaning "the productive imagination" is from 1580s. That of "a fanciful image or conception" is from 1660s. Meaning "fans of an amusement or sport, collectively" is attested by 1735, especially (though not originally) of the prize ring. The adjective is recorded from 1751 in the sense "fine, elegant, ornamental" (opposed to plain); later as "involving fancy, of a fanciful nature" (1800). Fancy man attested by 1811.

taste: c. 1300, "to touch, to handle," from Old French *taster* "to taste, sample by mouth; enjoy" (13c.), earlier "to feel, touch, pat, stroke" (12c., Modern French *tâter*), from Vulgar Latin *tastare*, apparently an alteration (perhaps by influence of *gustare*) of *taxtare*, a frequentative form of Latin *taxare* "evaluate, handle." Meaning "to take a little food or drink" is from c. 1300; that of "to perceive by sense of taste" is recorded from mid-14c.

Then, with intense eagerness, and with a courage not customary to him, he entered the shop and pointing with his horny finger to the "fruit" which had taken his fancy he asked the shopkeeper its price. The shopkeeper replied that a pound of the "fruit" would cost two cents.

Finding that the price was not at all high for what in his opinion was such a beautiful fruit, our Kurd decided to buy a whole pound.

Having finished his business in town, he set off again on foot for home the same day.

> **courage:** c. 1300, *corage*, "heart (as the seat of emotions)," hence "spirit, temperament, state or frame of mind," from Old French *corage* "heart, innermost feelings; temper" (12c., Modern French courage), from Vulgar Latin *coraticum* (source of Italian *coraggio*, Spanish *coraje*), from Latin *cor* "heart." Meaning "valor, quality of mind which enables one to meet danger and trouble without fear" is from late 14c. In this sense Old English had *ellen*, which also meant "zeal, strength." Words for "heart" are also common metaphors for inner strength. In Middle English, the word was used broadly for "what is in one's mind or thoughts," hence "bravery," but also "wrath, pride, confidence, lustiness," or any sort of inclination, and it was used in various phrases, such as *bold corage* "brave heart," *careful corage* "sad heart," *fre corage* "free will," *wikked corage* "evil heart."

Fruiterer, shopkeeper: Note that the term grocer is not used. A keeper is a warden. The shopkeeper is the warden of what is available for sale.

Horny finger: Fingers are not usually described as horny. If you look up the etymology of horny, it actually refers to the head. And it is used in *The Tales* to indicate reason; Beelzebub's reason at the end of *The Tales* is measured by the way that his horns grow. So the horny finger may be 'the finger of reason'. From sexual slang it could simply mean lustful.

> *in spite of his having scarcely any money*

Money is used to symbolize energy at several points throughout *The Tales*. Candidates for the Work can be regarded as poor in the *New Testament* sense of the word.

At Sunset

> *Walking at sunset over the hills and dales, and willynilly perceiving the exterior visibility of those enchanting parts of the bosom of Great Nature, the Common Mother, and involuntarily inhaling a pure air uncontaminated by the usual exhalations of industrial towns, our Kurd quite naturally suddenly felt a wish to gratify himself with some ordinary food also; so sitting down by the side of the road,... he took from his provision bag some bread and the "fruit" he had bought which had looked so good to him, and leisurely began to eat.*

At sunset: When, in *The Tales*, Gurdjieff refers to night and day, he's not usually referring to literal night and day, but metaphorically to waking sleep (night) and to consciousness (day). So sunset is the borderland between the two.

willynilly: c. 1600, contraction of "will I, nill I," or "will he, nill he," or "will ye, nill ye," literally "with or without the will of the person concerned."

Willy-nilly: He didn't have any choice, he's in the countryside, he sees the countryside, he starts to get impressions of the countryside. He is unable not to not observe it. He experiences pure foods of impressions and air, and commences to partake of another kind of food. He's "in essence," perhaps.

> *...he took from his provision bag some bread and the "fruit" he had bought which had looked so good to him, and leisurely began to eat.*

Bread: This is another New Testament symbol (two fish and five loaves of bread. Bread as the flesh of Christ, etc.). He eats bread with the "fruit." He invokes his spirit.

Provision bag: This is an odd choice of words. Provision indicates what is prepared for the future. So, metaphorically, *The Tales* is in our provision bag.

leisure: c. 1300, *leisir*, "free time, time at one's disposal," also (early 14c.) "opportunity to do something, chance, occasion, an opportune time," also "lack of hurry," from Old French *leisir*, variant of *loisir* "capacity, ability, freedom (to do something); permission; spare time; free will; idleness, inactivity," noun use of infinitive *leisir* "be permitted," from Latin *licere* "to be allowed" (see licence (n.)).

Horror of Horrors

> *But . . . horror of horrors! . . . very soon everything inside him began to burn. But in spite of this he kept on eating.*
>
> *And this hapless biped creature of our planet kept on eating,...*

Horror of horrors - the etymology of the word horror:

horror: early 14c., "feeling of disgust;" late 14c., "emotion of horror or dread," also "thing which excites horror," from Old French horror (12c., Modern French *horreur*) and directly from Latin "horror, dread, veneration, religious awe," a figurative use, literally "a shaking, trembling (as with cold or fear), shudder, chill," from *horrere* "to bristle with fear, shudder."

He starts to eat the red peppers and horror of horrors—religious awe, veneration, dread.

The words "hapless" and "biped" are curious choices. Hapless could simply be taken to mean unlucky, although there is nothing in the story of the Kurd to indicate that his purchase was unlucky. The etymology of *hap* is:

> **hap:** c. 1200, "chance, a person's luck, fortune, fate;" also "unforeseen occurrence," from Old Norse *happ* "chance, good luck," from Proto-Germanic *hap-* (source of Old English *gehæp* "convenient, fit"). Meaning "good fortune" in English is from early 13c. Old Norse seems to have had the word only in positive senses.

In this context, someone who is hapless might be someone who is not directly under the law of accident—laws of chance—but is instead influenced by the laws of fate. The word "biped," meaning two-footed, may imply to the Christian symbol of the foot as the point at which you interact with life. The left foot indicating essence and the right personality. Thus "hapless biped" might, metaphorically, indicate someone who is attracted to the Work (The Fool in the Tarot).

> *...thanks only to that particular human inherency which I mentioned at first, the principle of which I intended, when I decided to use it as the foundation of the new literary form I have created, to make, as it were, a "guiding beacon" leading me to one of my aims in view, and the sense and meaning of which moreover you will, I am sure, soon grasp—of course according to the degree of your comprehension—during the reading of any subsequent chapter of my writings, if, of course, you take the risk and read further, or, it may perhaps be that even at the end of this first chapter you will already "smell" something.*

Gurdjieff makes it clear that he is challenging the reader to dare to read the book. He emphasizes that it will be difficult, and that the difficulty he has created is a "guiding beacon" of his new literary form. Anyone who has struggled with *The Tales* knows full well that it is an entirely new literary form. We describe this form as best we can in the final chapter of this book.

Burning Inside

> *And so, just at the moment when our Kurd was overwhelmed by all the unusual sensations proceeding within him from this strange repast on the bosom of Nature, there came along the same road a fellow villager of his, one reputed by those who knew him to be very clever and experienced;*

> **repast:** late 14c., from Old French *repast* (Modern French *repas*) "a meal, food," from Late Latin *repastus* "meal" (also source of Spanish *repasto*,

noun use of past participle of *repascere* "to feed again," from Latin re- "repeatedly" (see re-) + *pascere* "to graze," from PIE root *pa-* "to feed." The verb (intransitive) is from late 15c.

The fellow villager is reputed to be clever and experienced—he recognizes what the Kurd is eating, "as if intent upon fulfillment of his most important duty," yet tells him to stop - perhaps because he is going against his nature. It is not our nature that requires us to work on ourselves, to develop Will. We satisfy the needs of Nature mechanically by our physical processes. The Kurd, however, chooses to struggle, and perhaps that is our most important duty.

> *and, seeing that the whole face of the Kurd was aflame, that his eyes were streaming with tears, and that in spite of this, as if intent upon the fulfillment of his most important duty, he was eating real "red pepper pods," he said to him:*

He starts to burn inside ("soon everything inside him began to burn"). His face is aflame, tears falling from his eyes. If you eat red pepper pods, possibly your nose will start to stream. You are unlikely to shed tears. You don't burn inside. Your cheeks don't go red (your face is not aflame). But if you experience true remorse, something like that may happen—the sun that neither lights nor heats may suddenly start to heat.

In a Paris meeting on December 7, 1941, Gurdjieff said (reportedly):

> *One needs fire. Without fire, there will never be anything. This fire is suffering, intentional suffering, without which it is impossible to create anything. One must prepare, must know what will make one suffer and when it is there, make use of it. Only you can prepare, only you know what makes you suffer, makes the fire which cooks, cements, crystallizes, DOES. Suffer by your defects, in your pride, in your egoism. Remind yourself of the aim. Without prepared suffering there is nothing, for by as much as one is conscious, there is no more suffering. No further process, nothing. That is why with your conscience you must prepare what is necessary. You owe to nature. The food you eat which nourishes your life. You must pay for these cosmic substances. You have a duty, an obligation, to repay by conscious work.*

This seems like a literal description of the metaphor Gurdjieff is using, when he refers to burning.

> *"What are you doing, you Jericho jackass? You'll be burnt alive! Stop eating that extraordinary product, so unaccustomed for your nature."*

A jackass is a male donkey. Christ rode a male donkey, a jackass, from Jericho to Jerusalem. That is most likely the Jericho Jackass Gurdjieff is referring to. By eating the red peppers, then, you may become the vehicle that carries the Christ within you towards the crucifixion.

The Last Two Cents

> But our Kurd replied: "No, for nothing on Earth will I stop. Didn't I pay my last two cents for them? Even if my soul departs from my body I shall still go on eating."

For nothing on earth would he stop eating - well, of course "for nothing on earth," possibly because there's "nothing on earth" he cares deeply about.

In none of the countries of Transcaucasia is the coinage cents. The 'two cents' probably refers to the widow's mites passage in *Mark 12:42-44* (a mite was a small coin, sometimes translated as a cent):

> And there came a certain poor widow, and she threw in two mites, which make a farthing. And he called unto him his disciples, and saith unto them, Verily I say unto you, That this poor widow hath cast more in, than all they which have cast into the treasury: For all they did cast in of their abundance; but she of her want did cast in all that she had, even all her living.

It is only at this point that the two cents are referred to as the "last two cents"— so everything he has.

> After what you have just perceived, I hope there may already be arising in your mentation a corresponding mental association which should, as a result, effectuate in you, as it sometimes happens to contemporary people, that which you call, in general, understanding, and that in the present case you will understand just why I, well knowing and having many a time commiserated with this human inherency, the inevitable manifestation of which is that if anybody pays money for something, he is bound to use it to the end, was animated in the whole of my entirety with the idea, arisen in my mentation, to take every possible measure in order that you, as is said "my brother in appetite and in spirit"—in the event of your proving to be already accustomed to reading books, though of all kinds, yet nevertheless only those written exclusively in the aforesaid "language of the intelligentsia"—having already paid money for my writings and learning only afterwards that they are not written in the usual convenient and easily read language, should not be compelled as a

*consequence of the said human inherency, to read my writings through
to the end at all costs, as our poor Transcaucasian Kurd was compelled
to go on with his eating of what he had fancied for its appearance
alone—that "not to be joked with" noble red pepper.*

Here Gurdjieff says that he has told this story as a warning to the reader who
might be tempted to buy his book, and then feel compelled to go on reading
to the end in order to get full value for money, not realizing the suffering he
may undergo, especially if Gurdjieff succeeds in his stated aim, "to destroy,
mercilessly…the beliefs and views…about everything existing…" He wants his
readers to be Transcaucasian Kurds, but not all readers will be.

*… it may perhaps be that even at the end of this first chapter you will
already "smell" something.*

"Smell" could be metaphorical, in the sense of smelling something out.
Curiously, it is related to the word "smoulder" - to burn inwardly.

Red pepper pods: The seeds Gurdjieff planted in *The Tales*.

The noble red pepper: Only here is the red pepper described as noble. High-
born, but not necessarily high-born in the sense of power-possessing, possibly
high-born in the religious sense.

Not to be joked with: *The Tales* is "not to be joked with" implying that the seeds
within the book are well above the level of humor.

*And so, for the purpose of avoiding any misunderstanding through
this inherency, the data for which are formed in the entirety of
contemporary man, thanks evidently to his frequenting of the cinema
and thanks also to his never missing an opportunity of looking into the
left eye of the other sex, I wish that this commencing chapter of mine
should be printed in the said manner, so that everyone can read it
through without cutting the pages of the book itself.*

The reference to the cinema is about passive entertainment that promotes
identification, as does television. We can find very little data about looking
into the left eye, aside from psychological studies, which suggest that we
normally look into the right eye (the eye of personality), rather than the left
eye (the eye of essence). It may be that left eye contact promotes sex, as the
words imply. In *In Search of the Miraculous* Gurdjieff is quoted as saying:

*"At the same time sex plays a tremendous role in maintaining the
mechanicalness of life. Everything that people do is connected with
'sex': politics, religion, art, the theater, music, is all 'sex.'"*

Gurdjieff is implying that readers may be inclined to read the book because they paid for it, simply and mechanically, by habit. And he wishes them to be able to return it, almost as if unread, in the hope of getting their money back.

Booksellers

> Otherwise the bookseller will, as is said, "cavil," and will without fail again turn out to act in accordance with the basic principle of booksellers in general, formulated by them in the words: "You'll be more of a simpleton than a fisherman if you let go of the fish which has swallowed the bait," and will decline to take back a book whose pages you have cut. I have no doubt of this possibility; indeed, I fully expect such lack of conscience on the part of the booksellers.

> And the data for the engendering of my certainty as to this lack of conscience on the part of these booksellers were completely formed in me, when, while I was a professional "Indian Fakir," I needed, for the complete elucidation of a certain "ultra-philosophical" question also to become familiar, among other things, with the associative process for the manifestation of the automatically constructed psyche of contemporary booksellers and of their salesmen when palming off books on their buyers.

> Knowing all this and having become, since the misfortune which befell me, habitually just and fastidious in the extreme, I cannot help repeating, or rather, I cannot help again warning you, and even imploringly advising you, before beginning to cut the pages of this first book of mine, to read through very attentively, and even more than once, this first chapter of my writings.

Books are no longer printed with pages uncut, and *The Tales* wasn't, even in its first printing. Gurdjieff here accuses booksellers of a lack of conscience, but realistically, if a book's pages have been cut, it is no longer pristine and the bookseller might be justified in refusing to take it back.

cavil: "to raise frivolous objections, find fault without good reason," 1540s, from Middle French *caviller* "to mock, jest," from Latin *cavillari* "to jeer, mock; satirize, argue scoffingly" (also source of Italian *cavillare*, Spanish *cavilar*), from *cavilla* "jest, jeering," which is related to *calumnia* "slander, false accusation."

"*You'll be more of a simpleton than a fisherman if you let go of the fish which has swallowed the bait,*"

The reference to fisherman is probably Biblical in the sense of Jesus promising to make his disciples "fishers of men." Those fishers of men were hardly simpletons in the normal sense. Gurdjieff then makes a curious statement about needing to become familiar with booksellers, in order to resolve an ultra-philosophical question. It seems unlikely that he is referring here to normal booksellers. It may be better understood as a bookseller being someone who simply trades in possible knowledge, but understands little themselves, being interested only in their personal profit. Such an individual would be likely to "cavil" about the return of a book.

> *The point is that in this fashionable language, the words "soul" and the bottom of your foot, also called "sole," are pronounced and even written almost alike.*

There is a nuance to Gurdjieff's philologizing about the English words "soul" and "sole"—the meaning of the word "sole" as an adjective. This is the etymology:

> **sole:** "single, alone, having no husband or wife; one and only, singular, unique," late 14c., from Old French soul "only, alone, just," from Latin *solus* "alone, only, single, sole; forsaken; extraordinary," of unknown origin, perhaps related to *se* "oneself."

If we review this passage in the German translations of *The Tales*, to see how the English element of it is handled, we see:

English soul is: „*englischen-Seele*". The words soul, "soul," and sole, "sole of the foot" are: *die Worte soul, „Seele," und sole, „Fußsohle."*

An interesting departure in idiom in this passage is: „*Mit-den-Wolfen-muß-man-heulen*"—literally "with the wolves you must howl" instead of "When you are in Rome do as Rome does,"

> *Now that you have become familiar with the story of our common countryman, the Transcaucasian Kurd, ...*

Our common countryman. This suggests that we all have a Transcaucasian Kurd—presumably essence.

From this point in the text, Gurdjieff launches into a discussion about the distinction between waking consciousness and the subconscious. Importantly he asserts that:

> *... in the writings following this chapter of warning I shall expound my thoughts intentionally in such sequence and with such "logical confrontation," that the essence of certain real notions may of*

189

> *themselves automatically, so to say, go from this "waking consciousness"—which most people in their ignorance mistake for the real consciousness, but which I affirm and experimentally prove is the fictitious one—into what you call the subconscious, which ought to be in my opinion the real human consciousness, and there by themselves mechanically bring about that transformation which should in general proceed in the entirety of a man and give him, from his own conscious mentation, the results he ought to have, which are proper to man and not merely to single- or double-brained animals.*

He promises the reader that his writing will have an impact, not just at the level of personality, but also at the level of essence, and that this "might, for the first time, compel you to reflect actively." He then proceeds to explain in detail about the two different forms of human consciousness.

The 1931 Manuscript

The 1931 Manuscript has a somewhat different and longer introduction to the tale of the Transcaucasian Kurd. Whereas in *The Tales* Gurdjieff simply mentions that he just remembered the story, and thought it useful to relate, in *The 1931 Manuscript*, he explains that his compulsion to carry out an idea at any cost was due to his hearing the tale:

> *The data engendering just this feature of my character, on account of which on all occasions, all kinds of factors for the formation of diverse for me personally "indigestible-consequences" always arise, were crystallized in my common presence from an impression perceived by me in my early youth, thanks to a story I heard about what happened to a certain "Transcaucasian Kurd."*

He goes on to say that he wasn't aware of this until later in life, after he had spent time following all the indications of the Yogis and studying "Psychoanalysis."

He explains that these data "evoke in me almost every time the experiencings called in ancient Indian philosophy 'commiseration-with-impartial-affection.' " Perhaps this corresponds to the "impulse of tenderness" mentioned in *The Tales.*

Two Cents/Six Groschen

The price of two cents for a pound of the fruit was "six-groschen" in *The 1931 Manuscript.* We read:

The shopkeeper replied that a pound of the fruit would cost "six-groschen".

"Groschen" is not an English word—the nearest equivalent in our language is the Old English "groat." The groschen was originally a small (15th century) silver coin used in Germany, Austria and elsewhere. In those days coins crossed international borders more easily, as they carried the intrinsic value of the metal from which they were pressed.

Even now, among older Germans, "groschen" indicates a coin of little value. A "groschen" is not a coin that a Transcaucasian Kurd would ever carry, and neither is a cent. This is anomalous. *The 1931 Manuscript* is made even more anomalous by the fact that Gurdjieff wraps "six-groshen" in quotes and hyphenates the words. English readers of *The Tales* would be unlikely to have any association with "six-groshen." Gurdjieff may have been referencing the following story. It originates from the Jewish tradition and is Russian in origin.

The Honest Blacksmith

Eliezer Reuven was a blacksmith who lived in the Russian town of Dobromysl. All day long he would stand by his forge, hammering the red-hot iron. He was honest and hard-working, and all the non-Jewish peasants who lived in the nearby villages respected him.

If their horses needed shoeing, they would bring them to the reliable blacksmith. If they needed a new axe, or their plough got broken, or the wheel on their wagon needed to be fixed, Eliezer Reuven was the best one to set things right.

One day, a peasant brought in his horse to get four new shoes, and at the same time another peasant brought in his wagon for repair. Then he too decided to have his horse shoed while he was there. Since the two jobs were very similar, Eliezer Reuven accidentally mixed up the amounts each man owed, so that one man paid too much, and the other too little. The difference between the two jobs, however, was only six groshen, a very small amount.

By the time Eliezer Reuven realized his mistake, both peasants had already gone home. The honest smith was so upset that he closed his shop, and set off on foot to refund the peasant's money. It was a hot summer's day, and the village was three miles off.

"I can't believe it!" a friend of Eliezer Reuven exclaimed. "You closed your shop and walked six miles in this heat just to return a few groshen! Why did you do that?"

> *"What do you expect?" Eliezer Reuven replied, "at the time of Noah's flood, people were so wicked that they would rob anyone of anything — even if it was worth less than a penny! Do you want me to be so much worse than they were, and rob a man of six whole groshen?"*

Gurdjieff probably made this change to *The 1931 Manuscript* because it had no impact on an English listener. We note that in the German edition of *The Tales* Gurdjieff preserves the "six-groschen," but does not wrap it in quotes. It reads:

> *Der Händler antwortete, daß ein Pfund dieser „Frucht" sechs Groschen koste.*

So Gurdjieff uses "six groshen," a German idiom for the German reader, which could be taken metaphorically to mean "the measure of an honest man."

Six groshen and two cents are both trivial amounts of money. In the English edition he prefers "two cents," an American idiom, derived from the English idiom "two pennies." Nowadays the expression "my two cents" or "my two pennies' worth" is a conventionally "humble" way to characterize one's opinion or advice. However, the origin of this phrase is probably from the "two mites" mentioned in The New Testament. It implies something distinctly different.

An Exhortation

The relating of the story of the Transcaucasian Kurd is similar, with some rewording, but in the middle, just before the fellow villager appears, *The 1931 Manuscript* includes an extra exhortation:

> *Meanwhile I boldly or, if you like, impudently, take it upon myself in advance to advise you to absorb with, as might be said, an "intensive-mobilization" of all your perceptive organs, the information elaborating the rest of this story, in order that the crystallization in you of the new impression may proceed normally and not in the manner in which it has already become habitual for this to proceed, that is to say, as the great sage Mullah Nassr Eddin defines and expresses it:*
>
> *"One part is used up for one's own welfare, and that only for today, while all the rest going in at one ear, is exhausted in the process of trying to get out at the other."*

Two Consciousnesses

In *The 1931 Manuscript* the whole passage on two consciousnesses is missing, with very little in its place. Gurdjieff simply makes the following statement in its stead:

... but I shall also touch upon questions from which there must inevitably arise unusual sensations and uncommon picturings in all your separate relatively independent parts, which parts the ancient sages characterized as "falsely-ascribing-initiative-to-themselves"; namely, in your thoughts, your feelings, and simply in your body.

He adds:

... I cannot do otherwise than as the most exalted great terrestrial sage Mullah Nassr Eddin would say, "tangle-and-entangle" the whole of you, or as he also sometimes says, "put-you-in-galoshes," in full face of the fact that I am counting on your help, or rather on your money, which I shall receive thanks to your purchase of writings; for the full possibility of accomplishing even with a "flourish," my self-imposed and perhaps from your point of view, purely egoistic aim.

10

Additional Advice To The Reader

"If you can put real attention on Beelzebub's Tales you can have real attention in life."

~ *Gurdjieff*

195

In this book we analyzed the first 27 pages of *The Tales*, stopping immediately prior to Gurdjieff's story about his grandmother's death. In the course of our analysis it became clear that this half of the first chapter focuses primarily on information the reader needs in order to read the book. We now review all of this material, beginning with Gurdjieff's initial advice:

> *I find it necessary on the first page of this book, quite ready for publication, to give the following advice:*
>
> *"Read each of my written expositions thrice:*
>
> *Firstly—at least as you have already become mechanized to read all your contemporary books and newspapers.*
>
> *Secondly—as if you were reading aloud to another person.*
>
> *And only thirdly—try and fathom the gist of my writings."*
>
> *Only then will you be able to count upon forming your own impartial judgment, proper to yourself alone, on my writings. And only then can my hope be actualized that according to your understanding you will obtain the specific benefit for yourself which I anticipate, and which I wish for you with all my being.*

Gurdjieff advises us to read the book in three different ways. Experience insists that we need to repeat each type of reading many times. The text does not "flow" in the customary way. Multiple readings in the second manner of reading are required to become familiar with the unusual rhythm of the words and to be able to articulate the sentences.

It is unlikely that many readers of the book will be skilled in reading (as if) aloud. Thus, in order to read the book as Gurdjieff advises, they will need to develop that skill. It is unprecedented and audacious to demand such a significant requirement from the reader. But there it is, staring out at you from a page of "Friendly Advice" that you encounter before the book begins.

Reading in the second way, you are reading (as if) for someone else. With the intellect you parse the words to comprehend what you are about to say. With the moving center your vocal chords speak the words. With the emotional center you moderate the sounds of the words as they are spoken (internally) to emphasize their meaning for the benefit of the (imaginary) reader.

This is subvocal speech. An Internet article entitled *Speaking to the Subconscious Using Subvocal Speech*[1] provides an insight into this process.

---

1. *https://itp.nyu.edu/classes/roy-spring2014/speaking-to-the-subconscious-using-subvocal-speech/*

Here is an excerpt:

> *Speech begins in the mind. Whether we say something out loud or silently to our self, we are still saying something. We may not move the air to sound it out but the muscles used to vocalize the words still receive a signal from the brain. This subvocal speech can be perceived through electromyography by measuring the electrical potential created by muscle cells in the throat when they receive a speech signal from the brain. Electrodes on the neck capture the subvocal speech and the silent communication is converted into audible speech.*
>
> *The simple human act of talking involves a complex set of systems. The science of speech is concerned with anatomy, neuroanatomy, physiology, and acoustics. Phonation is the production of sound during vocalization when muscle contractions in the larynx and the movement of breath are used to vibrate the vocal folds and modulate air flow from the lungs. But even when the acoustic aspects of phonation are removed we are still speaking in our head and the other systems of speech are still active. Activity in the muscle cells involved in the phonation of the words can be converted during silent thought to speech using subvocal recognition.*
>
> *The verbal mind has a strong attachment to speech. We listen to our thoughts, consciously and subconsciously, that are spoken quietly in the mind. And when we read we say the words silently in our head. Listening to your thoughts can feel like having a conversation with yourself. Silencing the subvocal voice is central to many traditions of religious and spiritual practice. Meditation is a tool for feeling equanimity towards your thoughts until the subvocal voice ceases to speak. But subvocalization is also used in many of the same traditions in the form of prayer where the subvocal voice is used to speak to God.*
>
> *Subvocal recognition technology is applied in circumstances when vocal communication is compromised or not possible. Pilots, astronauts, and divers can use subvocal speech to communicate with one another in conditions when vocal acoustic speech is not possible. Subvocal recognition was also developed by the military as a way of communicating during combat or hostage situations.*

For more, read the article on the web (see footnote on previous page).

The third way of reading, to "try and fathom the gist," is distinctly different in that here it is necessary, as Gurdjieff declares, to try (sit in judgement over) the text. In order to do this we will need to employ a series of techniques, which we itemized in Chapter 1:

1) View *The Tales* as a sacred book, as an objective work of art.

2) Consult the etymological meaning of the words.

3) Do not skip past any word that you do not understand.

4) Research all of Gurdjieff's real world references.

5) When considering meaning, take account of punctuation and typography—specifically: capitalization, quotes and concatenation.

6) The meaning of Gurdjieff's neologisms and his invented names needs to be decoded, no matter how difficult that proves to be.

7) We need to take note of and ponder intentional inexactitudes and odd word choices.

8) Use *The 1931 Manuscript* to help you to understand *The Tales*.

9) Reading *The Tales* is work on oneself.

10) Use *The Tales* to formulate questions and ponder the answers.

That is not everything. There is also the advice that Gurdjieff furnishes in *The Arousing of Thought*. Neither the first chapter of *The Tales* nor its last chapter, *From the Author*, which runs to 54 pages, refers directly to the contents of the book, except at one or two points. Mostly they both provide useful information on how to read the book in the third way.

In the final chapter we read:

> *Having now finished the first series of books, and, following the practice already long ago established on the Earth—never to conclude any great, as is said, "undertaking" without what some call an epilogue, others an afterword, and still others "from the author," and so on—I also now propose to write something of the same kind for them.*
>
> *With this end in view I very attentively read over this morning the "preface" I wrote six years ago entitled "The Arousing of Thought" in order to take corresponding ideas from it for a corresponding so to say "logical fusion" of that beginning with this conclusion which I now intend to write. [p1184]*

Also we read, as an introduction to the lecture that Gurdjieff includes in this chapter (THE VARIETY, ACCORDING TO LAW, OF THE MANIFESTATIONS OF HUMAN INDIVIDUALITY):

I append just this particular lecture, in the first place, because, at the very beginning of the dissemination of the ideas I imported into life, it was specially prepared here on the continent of Europe to serve as the introduction or, as it were, threshold for the whole series of subsequent lectures, by no less than the whole sum of which was it possible both to make clear in a form accessible to everybody the necessity and even the inevitability of a practical actualization of the immutable truths I have elucidated and established in the course of half a century of day-and-night active work and also to prove the actual possibility of employing those truths for the welfare of people; and secondly I append it here, because, while it was last being publicly read, and I happened myself to be present at that numerous gathering, I made an addition which fully corresponds to the hidden thought introduced by Mr. Beelzebub himself into his, so to say, "concluding chord," and which at the same time, illuminating once more this most great objective truth, will in my opinion make it possible for the reader properly to perceive and assimilate this truth as befits a being who claims to be an "image of God." [p1188-1189]

So here Gurdjieff claims that there is a hidden thought that Mr. Beelzebub introduces into his "concluding chord." For convenience, we print the "concluding chord" below.

Simultaneously 'something' pale yellow began little by little to arise around Beelzebub and to envelop Him, and it was in no way possible to understand or to discern whence this something issued—whether it issued from Beelzebub Himself or proceeded to Him from space from sources outside of Him.

Finding Himself in these cosmic actualizations incomprehensible for all three-brained beings, Beelzebub in a loud voice unusual for Him very penetratingly intoned the following words:

"THOU ALL and the ALLNESS of my WHOLENESS!

"The sole means now for the saving of the beings of the planet Earth would be to implant again into their presences a new organ, an organ like Kundabuffer, but this time of such properties that every one of these unfortunates during the process of existence should constantly sense and be cognizant of the inevitability of his own death as well as of the death of everyone upon whom his eyes or attention rests.

"Only such a sensation and such a cognizance can now destroy the egoism completely crystallized in them that has swallowed up the whole

of their Essence and also that tendency to hate others which flows from it—the tendency, namely, which engenders all those mutual relationships existing there, which serve as the chief cause of all their abnormalities unbecoming to three-brained beings and maleficent for them themselves and for the whole of the Universe." [p1183]

We cannot be sure as to what the hidden thought might be, but we suspect that it resides in the words: "Only such a sensation and such a cognizance..."

Mentation by Thought, Mentation by Form

The chapter, *From The Author*, includes the following useful description of the nature of Man. This is easier to comprehend if you read it slowly and carefully, trying to absorb all that it contains.

For one who desires to study human mechanicality in general and to make it clear to himself, the very best object of study is he himself with his own mechanicality; and to study this practically and to understand it sensibly, with all one's being, and not "psychopathically," that is, with only one part of one's entire presence, is possible only as a result of correctly conducted self-observation.

And as regards this possibility of correctly conducting self-observation and conducting it without the risk of incurring the maleficent consequences which have more than once been observed from people's attempts to do this without proper knowledge, it is necessary that the warning must be given—in order to avoid the possibility of excessive zeal—that our experience, based on the vast exact information we have, has shown that this is not so simple a thing as at first glance it may appear. This is why we make the study of the mechanicality of contemporary man the groundwork of a correctly conducted self-observation.

Before beginning to study this mechanicality and all the principles for a correctly conducted self-observation, a man in the first place must decide, once and forever, that he will be sincere with himself unconditionally, will shut his eyes to nothing, shun no results wherever they may lead him, be afraid of no inferences, and be limited by no previous, self-imposed limits; and secondly, in order that the elucidation of these principles may be properly perceived and transubstantiated in the followers of this new teaching, it is necessary to establish a corresponding form of "language," since we find the established form of language quite unsuitable for such elucidations. [p1209-1210]

Let us not dash past what Gurdjieff says here in clear unambiguous words: our current language is unsuitable for discussing these psychological topics, therefore we need to establish a form of language that is, otherwise we will get nowhere.

As regards the first condition, it is necessary now at the very outset to give warning that a man unaccustomed to think and act along lines corresponding to the principles of self-observation must have great courage to accept sincerely the inferences obtained and not to lose heart; and submitting to them, to continue those principles further with the crescendo of persistence, obligatorily requisite for this.

These inferences may, as is said, "upset" all the convictions and beliefs previously deep-rooted in a man, as well as also the whole order of his ordinary mentation; and, in that event, he might be robbed, perhaps forever, of all the pleasant as is said "values dear to his heart," which have hitherto made up his calm and serene life. [p1210-1211]

Gurdjieff states quite clearly that observing one's mechanicality is not for the faint-hearted. It is easy enough to accept one's mechanicality as a theory, but it is not so easy to observe it directly and accept it as reality.

Thanks to correctly conducted self-observation, a man will from the first days clearly grasp and indubitably establish his complete powerlessness and helplessness in the face of literally everything around him.

With the whole of his being he will be convinced that everything governs him, everything directs him. He neither governs nor directs anything at all.

He is attracted and repelled not only by everything animate which has in itself the capacity to influence the arising of some or other association in him, but even by entirely inert and inanimate things.

Without any self-imagination or self-calming—impulses which have become inseparable from contemporary men—he will cognize that his whole life is nothing but a blind reacting to the said attractions and repulsions.

He will clearly see how his what are called world-outlooks, views, character, taste, and so on are molded—in short, how his individuality was formed and under what influences its details are liable to change. [p1211]

For those who wish to ponder it, Gurdjieff describes without varnish what the state of normal man is and, in case you might wish to buffer it, the state of anyone in the Work prior to true efforts at self-observation.

> *And as regards the second indispensable condition, that is, the establishment of a correct language; this is necessary because our still recently established language which has procured, so to say, "rights-of-citizenship," and in which we speak, convey our knowledge and notions to others, and write books, has in our opinion already become such as to be now quite worthless for any more or less exact exchange of opinions.*
>
> *The words of which our contemporary language consists, convey, owing to the arbitrary thought people put into them, indefinite and relative notions, and are therefore perceived by average people "elastically."*
>
> *In obtaining just this abnormality in the life of man, a part was played in our opinion, by always that same established abnormal system of education of the rising generation.*
>
> *And it played a part because, based, as we have already said, chiefly on compelling the young to "learn by rote" as many words as possible differentiated one from the other only by the impression received from their consonance and not by the real pith of the meaning put into them, this system of education has resulted in the gradual loss in people of the capacity to ponder and reflect upon what they are talking about and upon what is being said to them. [p1211-1212]*

Our Systems of Education

The question for the reader of *The Tales* is whether he or she truly comprehends the negative effect of our systems of education that insist upon our learning by rote. We cannot sit idly by as disinterested observers to this, because we too were educated according to some such system and we too are (in almost all circumstances) victims of this kind of education. The assertion here is disturbing to say the least. It is this: because of our education we have largely lost the ability to ponder. And, incidentally, if we do not have that ability, we will **never** be able to read *The Tales* in the third way.

> *As a result of the loss of this capacity and in view, at the same time, of the necessity to convey thoughts more or less exactly to others, they*

203

are obliged, in spite of the endless number of words already existing in all contemporary languages, either to borrow from other languages or to invent always more and more words; which has finally brought it about that when a contemporary man wishes to express an idea for which he knows many apparently suitable words and expresses this idea in a word which seems, according to his mental reflection, to be fitting, he still instinctively feels uncertain whether his choice is correct, and unconsciously gives this word his own subjective meaning.

Owing on the one hand to this already automatized usage, and on the other hand to the gradual disappearance of the capacity to concentrate his active attention for any length of time, the average man on uttering or hearing any word involuntarily emphasizes and dwells upon this or that aspect of the notion conveyed by the word, invariably concentrating the whole meaning of the word upon one feature of the notion indicated by it; that is to say, the word signifies for him not all the implications of the given idea, but merely the first chance significance dependent upon the ideas formed in the link of automatic associations flowing in him. Hence every time that in the course of conversation the contemporary man hears or speaks one and the same word, he gives it another meaning, at times quite contradictory to the sense conveyed by the given word. [p1212-1213]

Making no attempt to soften the blow, Gurdjieff now suggests that we do not even know how to use words and how to select appropriate ones to convey what we wish to convey in conversation. We do not communicate, we only imagine that we do from our perch in our inner world.

For any man who has become aware of this to some degree, and has learned more or less how to observe, this "tragicomic feast of sound" is particularly sharply constated and made evident when others join the conversation of two contemporary people.

Each of them puts his own subjective sense into all the words that have become gravity-center words in the said so to say "symphony of words without content," and to the ear of this impartial observer it is all perceived only as what is called in the ancient Sinokooloopianian tales of The Thousand and One Nights, "cacophonous-fantastic-nonsense."

Conversing in this fashion, contemporary people nevertheless imagine they understand one another and are certain that they are conveying their thoughts to each other. [p1213]

Here it may make sense to discuss the meaning of words. Some words, for example, are practical: hammer, nail, screwdriver, knife and so on. When one person speaks to another about a hammer, perhaps giving instruction on how to use it effectively, the conversation is unlikely to go astray. One reason for this is context. What the instructor says, he will put into practice, or request his pupil to put into practice. If there is any misunderstanding it will become evident and it will be corrected. Moreover the instructor may well have a deep knowledge of hammers and their possibilities. When he or she says "hammer," the word is manifested from a detailed and coherent knowledge of hammers.

Now transfer the conversation to the topic of politics, with two people discussing how the economy of a particular country should be managed. The conversation heads for incoherence almost immediately. It is unlikely that either individual knows what an economy really is, or has any idea of the full set of techniques that can be employed in managing an economy. It is unlikely that either truly understands tax in all its forms, consumer behavior and its variation, the sectors of the economy, the impact of interest rate variations and so on. Nevertheless they believe they can have a coherent conversation around this topic and it is easy to imagine them disagreeing when in reality they agree or vice versa. They are pouring directly from the empty into the void and they enjoy doing so.

> *We, on the other hand, relying upon a mass of indisputable data confirmed by psycho-physico-chemical experiments, categorically affirm that as long as contemporary people remain as they are, that is to say "average people," they will never, whatever they may be talking about among themselves, and particularly if the subject be abstract, understand the same notions by the same words nor will they ever actually comprehend one another. [p1213]*

Abstract Thinking

It is important to understand that all conversations that are not practical are abstract to some degree. To understand abstraction is itself beyond the habitual capabilities of many people, because a genuine thinking effort is required to do even that.

> *This is why, in the contemporary average man, every inner experience and even every painful experience which engenders mentation and which has obtained logical results which might in other circumstances be very beneficent to those round about, is not*

manifested outwardly but is only transformed into so to say an "enslaving factor" for him himself. [p1213-1214]

This is the penalty. Trying to understand our own psyche alone is at least as difficult as understanding, say, carpentry, without help from another. We may have useful experiences that, if we could convey them to others, would genuinely help them. But if we have not the language we cannot be a good neighbor to them in this way, and should we be slightly inaccurate in our observations or conclusion about our experiences, then there is no-one to help us. It is possible then that those experiences become, as Gurdjieff says, an "enslaving factor."

> *Thanks to this, even the isolation of the inner life of each individual man is increased, and as a consequence what is called the "mutual instruction" so necessary to people's collective existence is always more and more destroyed.*
>
> *Owing to the loss of the capacity to ponder and reflect, whenever the contemporary average man hears or employs in conversation any word with which he is familiar only by its consonance, he does not pause to think, nor does there even arise in him any question as to what exactly is meant by this word, he having already decided, once and for all, both that he knows it and that others know it too. [p1214]*

As an example, let us here and now take the word "consonance." What do you think it means?

If you have read *The Tales* even once, you have definitely met with this word, even if you never encountered it before you read *The Tales*. In the text it occurs 13 times in the singular form (consonance) and 5 times in the plural form (consonances). It is possible that you will confuse the meaning of this word with the meaning of consonant, which is a letter of an alphabet that is not a vowel.

The dictionary definitions for this word are:

- agreement or compatibility between opinions or actions: consonance between conservation measures and existing agricultural practice.

- the recurrence of similar sounds, especially consonants, in close proximity (chiefly as used in prosody).

- Music the combination of notes that are in harmony with each other due to the relationship between their frequencies.

More light is shed on the meaning of the word when we consult the etymology:

> **consonance:** late 14c., "pleasing combination of sounds, harmony," from Old French *consonance* (12c.) "consonance, rhyme" and directly from Latin *consonantia* "harmony, agreement," from *consonantem* (nominative *consonans*) "agreeing in sound," present participle of *consonare* "to sound together, sound aloud." From early 15c. as "agreement among persons as to facts or opinions." Meaning "accord or agreement of sounds in words or syllables" is from 1580s.

If, by chance, you never had a strong understanding of the meaning of the word consonance, Gurdjieff now explains what process you may have gone through to arrive at whatever meaning you had assigned to that word.

> *A question, perhaps, does sometimes arise in him when he hears an entirely unfamiliar word the first time; but in this case he is content merely to substitute for the unfamiliar word another suitable word of familiar consonance and then to imagine that he has understood it.* [p1214]

Indeed.

Gurdjieff's Example

> *To bring home what has just been said, an excellent example is provided by the word so often used by every contemporary man— "world."*
>
> *If people knew how to grasp for themselves what passes in their thoughts when they hear or use the word "world," then most of them would have to admit—if of course they intended to be sincere—that the word carries no exact notion whatever for them. Catching by ear simply the accustomed consonance, the meaning of which they assume that they know, it is as if they say to themselves "Ah, world, I know what this is," and serenely go on thinking.*
>
> *Should one deliberately arrest their attention on this word and know how to probe them to find just what they understand by it, they will at first be plainly as is said "embarrassed," but quickly pulling themselves together, that is to say, quickly deceiving themselves, and recalling the first definition of the word that comes to mind, they will then offer it as their own, although, in fact, they had not thought of it before.*

If one has the requisite power and could compel a group of contemporary people, even from among those who have received so to say "a good education," to state exactly how they each understand the word "world," they would all so "beat about the bush" that involuntarily one would recall even castor oil with a certain tenderness. For instance, one of them who among other things had read up a few books on astronomy, would say that the "world" is an enormous number of suns surrounded by planets situated at colossal distances from each other and together forming what we call the "Milky Way"; beyond which, at immeasurable distances and beyond the limits of spaces accessible to our investigation, are presumably other constellations and other worlds.

Another, interested in contemporary physics, would speak of the world as a systematic evolution of matter, beginning with the atom and winding up with the very largest aggregates such as planets and suns; perhaps he would refer to the theory of the similitude of the world of atoms and electrons and the world of suns and planets, and so on in the same strain.

One who, for some reason or other, had made a hobby of philosophy and read all the mishmash on that subject would say that the world is only the product of our subjective picturings and imaginings, and that our Earth, for example, with its mountains and seas, its vegetable and animal kingdoms, is a world of appearances, an illusory world.

A man acquainted with the latest theories of polydimensional space would say that the world is usually looked upon as an infinite three-dimensional sphere, but that in reality a three-dimensional world as such cannot exist and is only an imagined cross section of another four-dimensional world out of which comes and into which goes everything proceeding around us.

A man whose world view is founded on the dogmas of religion would say that the world is everything existing, visible and invisible, created by God and depending on His Will. Our life in the visible world is brief, but in the invisible world, where a man receives reward or punishment for all his acts during his sojourn in the visible world, life is eternal.

One bitten with spiritualism would say that, side by side with the visible world, there exists also another, a world of the "Beyond," and that communication has already been established with the beings populating this world of the "Beyond."

A fanatic of theosophy would go still further and say that seven worlds exist interpenetrating each other and composed of more and more rarefied matter, and so on.

In short, not a single contemporary man would be able to offer a single definite notion, exact for all acceptances, of the real meaning of the word "world." [p1214-1216]

It may assist the reader if, when reading this passage, they try to observe their inner world behaving in the way described by Gurdjieff. At this specific point in the text Gurdjieff describes the inner life of the average man.

Our Automatism

The whole psychic inner life of the average man is nothing but an "automatized contact" of two or three series of associations previously perceived by him of impressions fixed under the action of some impulse then arisen in him in all the three heterogeneous localizations or "brains" contained in him. [p1216]

Here, Gurdjieff is unambiguous in his choice of words. "The whole psychic inner life of the average man..." He describes mechanicality ("automatized contact") between previously perceived and recorded associations and some impulse that has arisen in all three brains.

When the associations begin to act anew, that is to say, when the repetition of corresponding impressions appears, they begin to constate, under the influence of some inner or outer accidental shock, that in another localization the homogeneous impressions evoked by them begin to be repeated. [p1216]

We take this to mean that the remembered associations begin to act anew through resonance with corresponding impressions from an inner or outer "shock." The word "constate," used extensively by Gurdjieff, is French in origin. In French it means to establish, ascertain, verify or prove. We take it to have the meaning of "establish by agreement between parties" (in this context between three brains). Gurdjieff's choice of the word "shock" (meaning a sudden blow, an upsetting or surprising event) indicates an inner or outer discontinuity.

All the particularities of the world view of the ordinary man and the characteristic features of his individuality ensue, and depend on the sequence of the impulses proceeding in him at the moment of the

209

perception of new impressions and also on the automatism established for the arising of the process of the repetition of those impressions.

And it is this that explains the incongruity, always observed even by the average man during his passive state, in the several associations having nothing in common, which simultaneously flow within him. [p1216-1217]

Gurdjieff may be referring here to the incongruity of dreams—something of which the average man is most likely aware. However it also applies to the flow of thoughts most of the time—waking dreams, woven from the intersections of chains of associations.

The said impressions in the common presence of a man are perceived owing to the three, as it were, apparatuses in him—as there are apparatuses in general in the presences of all animals—acting as perceivers for all the seven what are called "planetary-gravity-center-vibrations."

The structure of these perceptive apparatuses is the same in all the parts of the mechanism.

They consist in adaptations recalling clean wax phonograph discs; on these discs, or, as they might otherwise be called, "reels," all the impressions received begin to be recorded from the first days after the appearance of a man in the world, and even before, during the period of his formation in his mother's womb.

And the separate apparatuses constituting this general mechanism possess also a certain automatically acting adaptation, owing to which newly arriving impressions, in addition to being recorded alongside those previously perceived and similar to them, are also recorded alongside those impressions perceived simultaneously with these latter. [p1217]

In other words, a threading together of impressions occurs between those recorded in the past, that are invoked by a current shock, and all the impressions that constitute the current shock.

Thus every impression experienced is inscribed in several places and on several reels, and there, on these reels, it is preserved unchanged.

These impressed perceptions have such a property that from contact with homogeneous vibrations of the same quality, they, so to say, "rouse themselves," and there is then repeated in them an action similar to the action which evoked their first arising.

210

And it is this repetition of previously perceived impressions engendering what is called association, and the parts of this repetition which enter the field of a man's attention, that together condition what is termed "memory." [p1217-1218]

So the way we respond to the new shock will be based on the way we responded to the initial impression. And all of these associations taken together are the memory of an average man.

The memory of the average man, in comparison with the memory of a man harmoniously perfected, is a very very imperfect adaptation for his utilization, during his responsible life, of his previously perceived store of impressions.

With the aid of memory, the average man from among impressions previously perceived can make use of and, so to say, keep track of only a very small part of his whole store of impressions, whereas the memory proper to the real man keeps track of all his impressions without exception, whenever they may have been perceived. [p1218]

Here Gurdjieff distinguishes between the average man and a man who has perfected himself. The average man's actions are performed entirely through this mechanism of a shock, invoking existing impressions from memory, leading to action based on previous action—in other words, predictable mechanical behavior.

The real man has at his disposal the whole of his memory and can choose how to act.

Many experiments have been made, and it has been established with indubitable exactitude, that every man in definite states, as for example in the state of a certain stage of hypnotism, can remember to the most minute particular everything that has ever happened to him; he can remember all the details of the surroundings and the faces and voices of the people around him, even those of the first days of his life, when he was still, according to people's notions, an unconscious being.

When a man is in one of these states, it is possible, artificially, to make even the reels hidden in the most obscure corners of the mechanism start working; but it often happens that these reels begin to unwind of themselves under the influence of some overt or hidden shock evoked by some experiencing, whereupon there suddenly rise up before the man long-forgotten scenes, picturings, faces, and so on. [p1218]

Back to *The Arousing of Thought*

What Gurdjieff described above is not the whole story. People make choices about how to earn their living, which friends to spend time with, which TV programs or movies to watch, and which books to read. In making such choices, (even if the choices they make are predestined by their mechanicality) they determine the contexts within which they will receive shocks to which they will respond mechanically. It may then be that some people are lucky, in that some shocks they receive come from B influence and pull them in the direction of C influence.

In *The Arousing of Thought*, Gurdjieff clearly describes two forms of mentation. He writes as follows:

> ... on Earth in the past it has been usual in every century that every man, in whom there arises the boldness to attain the right to be considered by others and to consider himself a "conscious thinker," should be informed while still in the early years of his responsible existence that man has in general two kinds of mentation: one kind, mentation by thought, in which words, always possessing a relative sense, are employed; and the other kind, which is proper to all animals as well as to man, which I would call "mentation by form."
>
> The second kind of mentation, that is, "mentation by form," by which, strictly speaking, the exact sense of all writing must be also perceived, and after conscious confrontation with information already possessed, be assimilated, is formed in people in dependence upon the conditions of geographical locality, climate, time, and, in general, upon the whole environment in which the arising of the given man has proceeded and in which his existence has flowed up to manhood.
>
> Accordingly, in the brains of people of different races and conditions dwelling in different geographical localities, there are formed about one and the same thing or even idea, a number of quite independent forms, which during functioning, that is to say, association, evoke in their being some sensation or other which subjectively conditions a definite picturing, and which picturing is expressed by this, that, or the other word, that serves only for its outer subjective expression.
>
> That is why each word, for the same thing or idea, almost always acquires for people of different geographical locality and race a very definite and entirely different so to say "inner content."

In other words, if in the entirety of any man who has arisen and been formed in any locality, from the results of the specific local influences and impressions a certain "form" has been composed, and this form evokes in him by association the sensation of a definite "inner content," and consequently of a definite picturing or notion for the expression of which he employs one or another word which has eventually become habitual, and as I have said, subjective to him, then the hearer of that word, in whose being, owing to different conditions of his arising and growth, there has been formed concerning the given word a form of a different "inner content," will always perceive and of course infallibly understand that same word in quite another sense.

This fact, by the way, can with attentive and impartial observation be very clearly established when one is present at an exchange of opinions between persons belonging to two different races or who arose and were formed in different geographical localities. [p15-17]

Gurdjieff is emphatic "... it has been usual in every century that every man, in whom there arises the boldness to attain the right to be considered by others and to consider himself a 'conscious thinker.'" His words suggest that we cannot simply become conscious thinkers by wanting it or pretending to it. To achieve it we need to master mentation by thinking, while also removing any negative influence that emerges from our mentation by form.

In *In Search of The Miraculous*, we read the following:

"For exact understanding exact language is necessary. And the study of systems of ancient knowledge begins with the study of a language which will make it possible to establish at once exactly what is being said, from what point of view, and in what connection. This new language contains hardly any new terms or new nomenclature, but it bases the construction of speech upon a new principle, namely, the principle of relativity; that is to say, it introduces relativity into all concepts and thus makes possible an accurate determination of the angle of thought—for what precisely ordinary language lacks are expressions of relativity.

"When a man has mastered this language, then, with its help, there can be transmitted and communicated to him a great deal of knowledge and information which cannot be transmitted in ordinary language even by using all possible scientific and philosophical terms.

"The fundamental property of the new language is that all ideas in it are concentrated round one idea, that is, they are taken in their mutual

relationship from the point of view of one idea. This idea is the idea of evolution. Of course, not evolution in the sense of mechanical evolution, because such an evolution does not exist, but in the sense of a conscious and volitional evolution, which alone is possible.

"Everything in the world, from solar systems to man, and from man to atom, either rises or descends, either evolves or degenerates, either develops or decays. But nothing evolves mechanically. Only degeneration and destruction proceed mechanically. That which cannot evolve consciously—degenerates. Help from outside is possible only in so far as it is valued and accepted, even if it is only by feeling in the beginning.

"The language in which understanding is possible is constructed upon the indication of the relation of the object under examination to the evolution possible for it; upon the indication of its place in the evolutionary ladder. [p77]

People who are experienced in the Work will recognize that they already use their native language (to some degree) in the way Gurdjieff describes. They have assigned different meanings to many common words and phrases: consciousness, considering, identification, mechanicality, waking sleep, and so on. In our view, the reader of *The Tales* needs to go further than this, and comprehend every word in the text through mentation by thought. The realization the reader sometimes (perhaps even frequently) experiences, on reading a sentence from the book, that they have never before understood the sentence and yet have happily moved past it in many readings of the book, may provide them with sufficient incentive to make the necessary effort. Such effort pays.

The Languages in Which *The Tales* Was Written

Gurdjieff declares clearly how *The Tales* was written in the first paragraph of the book:

Original written in Russian and Armenian. Translations into other languages have been made under the personal direction of the author, by a group of translators chosen by him and specially trained according to their defined individualities, in conformity with the text to be translated and in relation to the philological particularities of each language.

The reader will possibly be curious as to why this matters. For the record, it is worth recounting here what is known of how he wrote the book.

In *Our Life With Mr Gurdjieff*, Olga de Hartmann writes:

> *From the time Mr Gurdjieff began to write "Beelzebub," he continued almost without stopping, day and night, at the café at Fontainebleau, the Café de la Paix in Paris, which was his "Headquarters," and during his trips. He wrote himself or dictated to me. Then I had to type it. He corrected, and then I had to retype again and again, sometimes as often as ten times. When he found that the Russian text had taken the form he wished, Mr de Hartmann would translate into "English" literally, word by word, with a dictionary; then it went to Mr Orage, who put it into real English. Then I checked this first translation with Mr Orage against the Russian text and after that we read it to Mr Gurdjieff.*

As regards the Armenian portions of the text, it was dictated to Lily Chaverdian, who typed in Armenian. The Armenian text was later translated into Russian, which was translated into English text, word for word. When Orage wasn't present at The Prieuré, Bernard Metz (and possibly others) put the text into a readable English form, and it was then sent to Orage in New York for further editing. Some of this editing work was also done by Jean Toomer.

In *The Arousing of Thought* Gurdjieff appears to agonize over the choice of language in which to write. There have been very few authors who were sufficiently skilled in more than one language to even consider such a question, so it is difficult for the reader to consider in a meaningful way. Nevertheless Gurdjieff has a good deal to say on the subject, using it to criticize both the Russian and English languages:

> *Both these languages are like the dish which is called in Moscow "Solianka," and into which everything goes except you and me, in fact everything you wish, and even the "after-dinner Cheshma" of Scheherazade.*

In our view the "except you and me" implies that neither language is suited to discussing psychological matters. Gurdjieff chose Armenian for that purpose.

Note that he comments on the consequences of using his automatism in both Russian and Armenian in the following way:

> *Adopting in the same given instance this popular wisdom formed by centuries and expressed by a stick, which, as was said, indeed has two ends, one end of which is considered good and the other bad, then if I use the aforesaid automatism which was acquired in me thanks only to long practice, it will be for me personally of course very good, but*

according to this saying, there must result for the reader just the opposite; and what the opposite of good is, even every non-possessor of hemorrhoids must very easily understand.

Briefly, if I exercise my privilege and take the good end of the stick, then the bad end must inevitably fall "on the reader's head."

The implication is that, for the sake of the reader, he did not employ his automatism.

Since the reader is (most likely) reading in English, we must revisit the question of why it matters what language the book was written in. This would seem to be especially the case if we have no knowledge at all of either Russian or Armenian.

With no experience of the mentation by form of a Russian or an Armenian, we will not be constrained by that. Instead we will be constrained by our personal English mentation by form. This will also be inappropriate for the text, even though the English version makes extensive use of English idioms. We have been thoroughly warned about such mentation by Gurdjieff anyway.

He may also be warning the reader that some of the words he used have no equivalent in English, and hence he has employed appropriate literary mechanisms (long clauses, concatenation, etc.) to convey meaning. Many of the neologisms that occur in the text derive from Russian or Armenian, but that is not the case for all of them.

Our best guess is that Gurdjieff devoted so many words in *The Arousing of Thought* to the discussion of languages specifically because it might arouse thought in the reader about the difficulty of conveying meaning in an objective way.

We can perhaps allow Louise March, Gurdjieff's principal collaborator in producing the German edition of *The Tales*, to have the final word here. She used the following words to describe her editorial work with Gurdjieff (from *The Gurdjieff Years 1929-1949 Recollections of Louise Goepfert March* by Annabeth McCorkle):

. . . he considered a single word or the flow of a sentence so very important, but we translators already knew Gurdjieff as "the teacher of exactness." For us, the translation was a school that freed us from our subjective conceptions and views. Thanks to the creation of a new, exact language, we came to an understanding which we couldn't have imagined in the beginning.

With Gurdjieff we came to use words precisely.

Grammar and the Bon Ton Literary Language

Gurdjieff expends considerable words warning the reader that he will not be writing in the manner that other writers write—in particular he will not be employing modern grammar. He writes:

> *I have the honor to inform you that although owing to circumstances that have arisen at one of the last stages of the process of my life, I am now about to write books, yet during the whole of my life I have never written not only not books or various what are called "instructive-articles," but also not even a letter in which it has been unfailingly necessary to observe what is called "grammaticality," and in consequence, although I am now about to become a professional writer, yet having had no practice at all either in respect of all the established professional rules and procedures or in respect of what is called the "bon ton literary language," I am constrained to write not at all as ordinary "patented-writers" do, to the form of whose writing you have in all probability become as much accustomed as to your own smell.*
>
> *This understanding of mine bids me inwardly to make the center of gravity of my warning my ignorance of the literary language.*

As we have observed, in *The Tales* Gurdjieff employs a grammar of association (quite likely his personal invention), which is both unusual and difficult to adjust to. The challenge for the reader is to learn to read and profit from this grammar.

It is possible that Gurdjieff's text is providing us with appropriate associations on every topic he addresses. It also appears to be the case that Gurdjieff plants specific associations for us to stumble across which relate one part of his whole series of books to another part. We have, for example, found sentences in *Meetings With Remarkable Men* which associate directly to sentences in *The Tales*. It may be that his advice on reading his books in order is because of the way that the associations may act upon us.

Allegory

In telling his first tale, the story of The Transcaucasian Kurd, Gurdjieff introduces us to an allegory constructed in a precise and detailed manner, indicating, among other things, that he will, throughout *The Tales*, use specific symbols (often New Testament symbols) to convey meaning in a way that Western literature rarely does.

In the first chapter of *Meetings with Remarkable Men* (the Introduction) Gurdjieff includes a long essay discussing language and grammar. We quote a brief extract here:

> '*This artificially invented grammar of the languages of today, which the younger generation everywhere is now compelled to learn, is in my opinion one of the fundamental causes of the fact that, among contemporary European people, only one of the three independent data necessary for obtaining a sane human mind has developed—namely, their so-called thought, which tends to predominate in their individuality; whereas without feeling and instinct, as every man with a normal reason must know, the real understanding accessible to man cannot be formed.*
>
> '*To sum up everything that has been said about the literature of our times, I cannot find better words to describe it than the expression "it has no soul."*
>
> '*Contemporary civilization has destroyed the soul of literature, as of everything else to which it has turned its gracious attention.*

The point here is that, aside from a grammar of logical associations that may convey meaning to the reader, in our view, Gurdjieff has included within his writings a grammar of symbols, which is also associative.

We here note the following words from *The Arousing of Thought*.

> *Now that you have become familiar with the story of our common countryman, the Transcaucasian Kurd, I already consider it my duty to make a confession and hence before continuing this first chapter, which is by way of an introduction to all my further predetermined writings, I wish to bring to the knowledge of what is called your "pure waking consciousness" the fact that in the writings following this chapter of warning I shall expound my thoughts intentionally in such sequence and with such "logical confrontation," that the essence of certain real notions may of themselves automatically, so to say, go from this "waking consciousness"—which most people in their ignorance mistake for the real consciousness, but which I affirm and experimentally prove is the fictitious one—into what you call the subconscious, which ought to be in my opinion the real human consciousness, and there by themselves mechanically bring about that transformation which should in general proceed in the entirety of a man and give him, from his own conscious mentation, the results he*

ought to have, which are proper to man and not merely to single- or double-brained animals.

The Requisite Effort

– Reference the dictionary meaning of all words when you are at all uncertain of the meaning. This begins the effort to create your own language for mentation by thought.

– Examine the etymological meaning of all words. This strengthens the understanding of individual words.

– When reading, never skip past any word, sentence or paragraph. Make notes at every place where you know you need to make more effort or do more research.

– Research all of Gurdjieff's real world references. Find out the meaning of everything he mentions.

– Take note of all typographic and punctuation conventions used:
  • full capitalization
  • initial capitalization
  • ellipsis
  • concatenation
  • quotes (in particular determine why quotes were used).

– Take note of and ponder intentional inexactitudes and odd or unusual word choices.

– Attempt to determine the meaning of Gurdjieff's neologisms and his invented names. At least make an attempt to do this.

– Take note of all repetitions. They are probably meant to have a hypnotic effect.

– Ponder. For example, Gurdjieff's discussion of languages: why does he discuss this topic?

– Follow and ponder all Gurdjieff's associations, embracing his strange "grammar." This becomes food for mentation by thought, and may additionally enrich one's mentation by form. They become your own material.

– Align with Gurdjieff's grammar of associations in respect of symbols. These become food for feeling.

Appendix: The Threads of *The Tales*

"A real work of art is as precise as a treatise on mathematics."

~ *Gurdjieff*

—⟋⟍—

The Threads of *The Tales*

Here we list without comment the various threads of *The Tales* first in respect of the individual stories or themes that make up each chapter, and also the various arcs (major themes) of *The Tales*.

Note that *The Tales* can be considered from the perspective of any and every cosmos. It will profit the reader to bear this in mind when trying to fathom the gist.

Individual Tales

This list divides *The Tales* up into its individual stories or episodes. Some are whole chapters; others are sections of a chapter. In some instances we encounter a tale within a tale.

Chapter 1. *The Arousing Of Thought*

The warning.

Which language to write in.

The Transcaucasian Kurd.

Cutting the pages of the book.

The death of Gurdjieff's grandmother.

The wisdom tooth.

All universal principle of living.

The choice of Beelzebub as hero.

Karapet of Tiflis.

Chapter 2. *Introduction: Why Beelzebub Was In Our Solar System*

The tale of Beelzebub's exile and his journey to Revozvradendr.

Chapter 3. *The Cause Of The Delay In The Falling Of The Ship Karnak*

The Madcap comet and Zilnotrago.

The inhabitants of the planets of the solar system Ors.

The Captain's story.

Chapter 4. *The Law Of Falling*

The tale of St. Venoma and his constatation of The Law of Falling.

The system of Saint Venoma.

Chapter 5. *The System Of Archangel Hariton*

The system of Archangel Hariton.

225

from Earth could ever understand cosmic laws.

The tale of Theophany.

Choon-Kil-Tez and Choon-Tro-Pel.

The Alla-Attapan.

The Lav-Merz-Nokh.

Chai-Yoo and his theory.

The Chinese and Greek octave of vibrations.

Chapter 41. *The Bokharian Dervish Hadji-Asvatz-Troov*

Hadji-Zephir-Bogga-Eddin and Hadji-Asvatz-Troov.

Hadji-Asvatz-Troov and his Sheikh's request.

The cave of Hadji-Asvatz-Troov.

The two causes of sound.

Hadji-Asvatz-Troov's experimental demonstration.

The European traveler, the electricity and gas in the cave.

Chapter 42. *Beelzebub In America*

The American businessman and his dollar businesses.

The "incantation" of Professor Kishmenhof.

The New York Restaurant.

The School of languages of Mr. Chatterlitz.

Beelzebub meets Mr. Bellybutton in Chicago.

The Chicago slaughterhouses and advertising.

American food preservation.

American wheat and prosphora.

The appendix.

The Tikliamishian civilization and the comfortable couch-bed.

The tale of Brother Asiman.

The spread of venereal disease in Europe and America.

The young Persian and the custom of abdest.

Prostitution, women females and women mothers.

The custom of Sooniat.

The Russian Orthodox Christians and the Lent fast.

The Kelnuanian council.

Customs of self-fumigation.

The tale of Sonya.

Major and Minor Arcs

Note that the following list of the themes has no implied order and may not be an exhaustive list:

The Redemption or Evolution of Beelzebub. Beelzebub guilty of sins committed in his youth is exiled to Ors and, by his deeds, he gradually redeems himself.

The Oskiano of Hassein. Hassein is gradually educated by his grandfather's stories, We can observe the gradual impact this has upon him from the text.

The Journey of the Karnak. The journey proceeds initially from Beelzebub's home planet, Karatas, eventually ending at Deskaldino. In studying this journey, we may like to include the various activities of the passengers on the Karnak.

The Heavenly Host. We can study the appearances, actions and explanations of various high individuals; angels, archangels, cherubim and seraphim.

Beelzebub's Sojourns. We can examine what prompted each sojourn and how Beelzebub interfered in the affairs of men.

Transspace Ships. This particular area of study involves considering the meaning of the various forms of locomotion of the transspace ships and the meaning of Karnak, Omnipresent and Occasion.

Saturn and Mars. Beelzebub's various activities on Saturn and Mars constitute a series of events for study.

The Descent of Mankind. While Beelzebub and Hassein evolve, in contrast, the situation of mankind gradually deteriorates.

HIS ENDLESSNESS and The Creation. Aside from the chapter on The Holy Planet "Purgatory," comments on The Heropass and HIS ENDLESSNESS are found at many points throughout *The Tales*.

Objective Science. There are many references throughout *The Tales* to the nature of Objective Science. There are many subsidiary arcs, including: Trogoautoegocrat, Heptaparaparshinokh, Triamazikamno, Laws, etc.

Messengers from Above. The various attempts by messengers from above to assist mankind.

The Hidden Arc. There is a hidden arc in *The Tales* which will eventually reveal itself to the attentive reader. This is all we intend to say about this.

BIBLIOGRAPHY

This is the full list of books consulted by the author in producing this book:

Perspectives on Beelzebub's Tales, by Keith A. Buzzell

Gurdjieff's Whim, by Keith A. Buzzell

Our Life with Mr. Gurdjieff, by Thomas and Olga de Hartmann

The Herald of Coming Good, by G. I. Gurdjieff

Beelzebub's Tales to His Grandson: All and Everything: 1st Series, by G. I. Gurdjieff

Meetings with Remarkable Men, by G. I. Gurdjieff

Life Is Real Only Then, When 'I Am', by G. I. Gurdjieff

Transcripts of Gurdjieff's Meetings: 1941-1946, published by Book Studio, London

Paris Meetings 1943, by G. I. Gurdjieff

Gurdjieff's Early Talks 1914-1931, by G. I. Gurdjieff and Joseph Aziz

Views from the Real World: Early Talks, by G. I. Gurdjieff

Diary of Madam Egout Pour Sweet, by Rina Hands

The New Man, by Maurice Nicoll

The Mark, by Maurice Nicoll

The Teachings of Gurdjieff, by C. S. Nott

A. R. Orage's commentaries on G. I. Gurdjieff's All and Everything: Beelzebub's Tales to His Grandson, by A. Orage and edited by C. S. Nott

In Search of the Miraculous, by Peter Ouspensky

Gurdjieff and the Women of the Rope: Notes of Meetings in Paris and New York 1935-1939 and 1948-1949, by Solita Solano (Contributor), Kathryn C. Hulme (Contributor)

G.I.Gurdjieff: A New Life, by Paul Beekman Taylor

Gurdjieff and Orage, by Paul Beekman Taylor

Gurdjieff's Invention of America, by Paul Beekman Taylor

The Philosophy of G.I.Gurdjieff - Time, Word and Being in "All and Everything", by Paul Beekman Taylor

Mister Gurdjieff's Hapax Legomena, by Nicolas Tereschenko

Guide and Index to G. I. Gurdjieff's Beelzebub's Tales to His Grandson, edited by Louise Welch and published by Traditional Studies Press in Toronto.

AUTHOR'S BIOGRAPHICAL NOTES

Robin Bloor was born in 1951 in Liverpool, UK. He obtained a BSc in Mathematics at Nottingham University and took up a career in the computer industry, initially writing software. From 1989 onwards, he became a technology analyst and consultant. He has thus been a writer of a kind ever since. In 2002 he was awarded an honorary Ph.D. in Computer Science by Wolverhampton University in the UK. He currently resides in and works from Austin, Texas in the USA.

In 1988, after drifting through several work groups, Bloor met and became a pupil of Rina Hands. Rina was a one-time associate of J. G. Bennett, a student of Peter Ouspensky's, and later, a pupil of George Gurdjieff. Following Gurdjieff's death, she remained part of J. G. Bennett's group for a while. Subsequently, she formed groups both in London, where she lived, and in Bradford in the North of England—initially in conjunction with Madame Nott. She was an accomplished movements teacher and an inspirational group leader. She died in 1994 and is buried next to Jane Heap in a cemetery in North London.

Bloor leads a group, The Austin Gurdjieff Society, in Austin, Texas. Aside from the usual movements and Work activities, the group specializes in the study of Gurdjieff's writings and the study of Objective Science, as articulated by Ouspensky in *In Search of The Miraculous*, and by Gurdjieff in *The Tales*.

He has written or edited six books about the Work, including the present volume. Details of his other books are provided on the following pages.

ACKNOWLEDGEMENTS

The author acknowledges the following individuals, who – whether they realize it or not – were of assistance in writing and publishing this book, and to whom he is grateful:

Paula Schmidt, who edited the book and made contributions to the text; Roderick Thorn, a member of Paula's Tales Study Group, who also made useful contributions; Jude Bloor, who participated in the editing process; all the members of the Austin Gurdjieff Society, who participated in many meetings where readings of *The Tales* and discussion of the text took place; all members of The Bradford Gurdjieff Society in the UK, particularly its leaders, Ron Jennings and Pauline Dickes; Paul Beekman Taylor, an author and friend; and, of course, Rina Hands, who was and remains an inspiration.

To Fathom The Gist Volume I
Approaches to the Writings of G I Gurdjieff

Unheralded and unexpected, *To Fathom The Gist* sparked renewed interest in Gurdjieff's objective literary masterpiece. Rather than a collection of thoughts or theories on the meaning of *Beelzebub's Tales*, this book is no more nor less than a well written guide on how to read the book productively. It provides a clear and concise description, with abundant examples, of a series of techniques a reader of *The Tales* can employ to better understand the book. Providing explanatory examples, it discusses: intellectual postures and processes, Gurdjieff's style and use of language, intentional inexactitudes in the text, the importance of etymology, Gurdjieff's use of neologisms, the need for background research into the content, the use of allegory, Gurdjieff's use of "egoplastikoori" and also objective science and its divergence from modern science.

The book has been described as: "Insightful and original," "Essential reading for anyone studying Gurdjieff's writings," "A True companion to All and Everything," "Valuable to any student of The Tales," "An ultra-effort" and "Exceptional." It has made a profound impact on many of its readers and has inspired the organization of study groups focussing on Gurdjieff's literature both in North America and Europe.

It is a seminal work, the foremost book written to assist those who wish to "fathom the gist" of Gurdjieff's objective literature - and it is likely to remain so for many years.

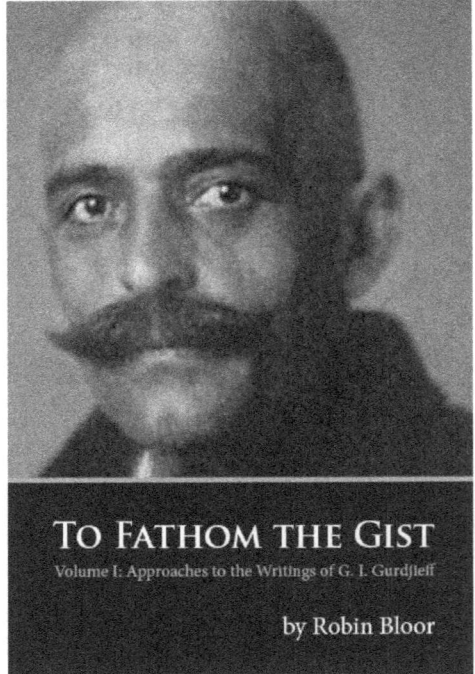

TO FATHOM THE GIST
Volume I: Approaches to the Writings of G. I. Gurdjieff

by Robin Bloor

TO FATHOM THE GIST VOLUME II
The Arch-Absurd

It might be expected that the second volume of *To Fathom The Gist* would continue in the direction forged by the first volume, but go a little further. It does not. Instead the author chose to investigate *The Tales* in a different way. He tried to envisage himself in Mr Gurdjieff's position and investigated the book from the perspective of the author. In essence, the theory behind this book is: "the more we can find out about how Gurdjieff wrote the book, the better we will be able to understand it."

As with the previous volume in this series, the book is alive with revelations about the meaning of various passages, given en passant as examples when the author explains aspects of how he believes the book was written, and also how Gurdjieff intended the book to be read. The book investigates Gurdjieff's philology in depth, not through intent, but because wherever the author turned he seemed to barge into it.

At times he was obliged to study both the German and French versions of *The Tales* to identify style and word choice variations between languages. He compared the 1931 private edition to the 1950 edition to identify compositional and editing changes. He conducted a thorough review of the much (and it seems rightly) criticized 1992 version of *The Tales*.

All of this activity leaps from the pages of the book, as the reader moves from chapter to chapter, enticing him or her to try and fathom the gist of Gurdjieff's masterpiece.

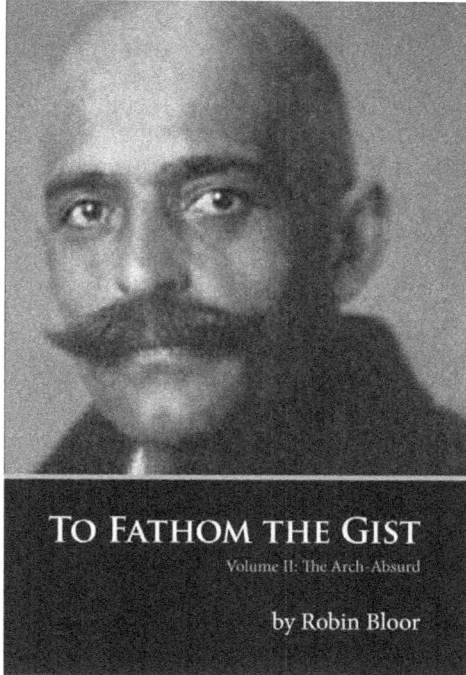

THE HERALD OF COMING GOOD:
First appeal to contemporary Humanity
[with notes]

The Herald of Coming Good: First appeal to contemporary Humanity was published in 1933, apparently as a precursor to the launch of Gurdjieff's magnum opus: *An Objectively Impartial Criticism of The Life of Man or Beelzebub's Tales to His Grandson.* However that book was not published until 1950. It was written in a difficult obtuse style, similar to that of his magnum opus.

THE HERALD OF COMING GOOD
FIRST APPEAL TO CONTEMPORARY HUMANITY
[WITH NOTES]

G. GURDJIEFF

It is a mysterious publication. It masquerades as a marketing booklet for attracting people to the Work, with registration blanks for readers to fill in, should they wish to subscribe to the books of the First Series. The casual reader was unlikely to make much sense of it.

Nevertheless, serious readers of Gurdjieff's writings may find its contents valuable. This version of the book has been "translated" into American English and also includes a rendering of the prospectus for Gurdjieff's Institute for the Harmonious Development of Man. As an adjunct to the book, there are some notes about *The Herald* made by the editor of this publication. They do not constitute a complete analysis. Nevertheless, they may prove useful to the reader.

THE 1931 MANUSCRIPT
OF
BEELZEBUB'S TALES TO HIS GRANDSON

This book is a thoroughly edited version of the original 1931 manuscript of *Beelzebub's Tales to His Grandson* by G. Gurdjieff. The text is, for the most part, unchanged from the original manuscript that was published in a limited edition in 1931 under the direction of A. R. Orage. However some editing to the text has been done to remove obvious typographical errors and to harmonize the spelling of Gurdjieff's many invented names and neologisms to align with the later published version of this classic literary work.

In addition, a full index is provided, almost to the level of a concordance. It documents all changes to the neologisms and all edits, aside from typo-graphical corrections made to the text. The attraction of this publication lies in the fact that, although Gurdjieff approved this original edition for publication and hence regarded his writing effort as almost complete, he subsequently made significant changes to many parts of it. As a consequence, reading *The 1931 Manuscript* at times feels as though one is reading a different book, but one that nevertheless bears the mark of its author.

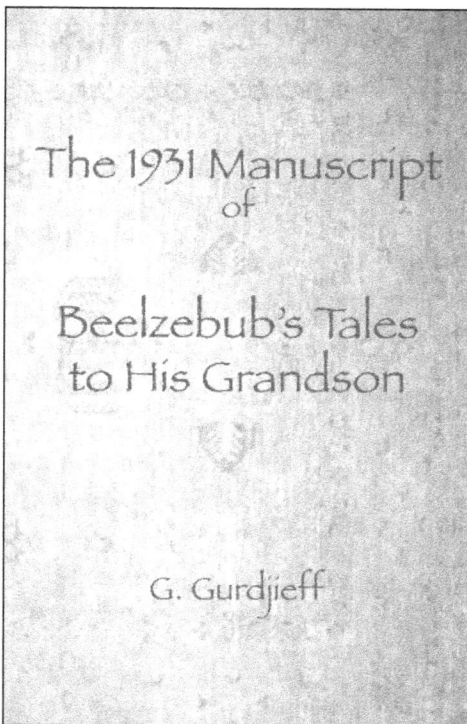

THE SEARCHABLE INDEX
TO G. I. GURDJIEFF'S
BEELZEBUB'S TALES TO HIS GRANDSON

This ebook provides a productive means for searching through, reading, and pondering the meaning of *Beelzebub's Tales To His Grandson* by G. I. Gurdjieff. It has been written and compiled by Robin Bloor, the author of *To Fathom The Gist, Volumes I and II*, to assist in some of the methods to fathoming the gist of *Beelzebub's Tales* described in those books. It is likely to prove useful to anyone who studies *The Tales* in depth, since the indexes and lists it includes are likely to be thought-provoking for the reader.

Words (including Gurdjieff's neologisms) that the compiler considered important or significant are organized into a comprehensive set of categories and arranged within those categories. There are about a hundred such categories covering everything from names of people and places to psychic states.

It could be thought of as a "digital concordance" as it includes the full text of *The Tales* and an index of every word used in *The Tales*, along with the frequency of its occurrence. However, note that it includes no references to the physical pages of any printed version of the book. It is not a true concordance in that sense.

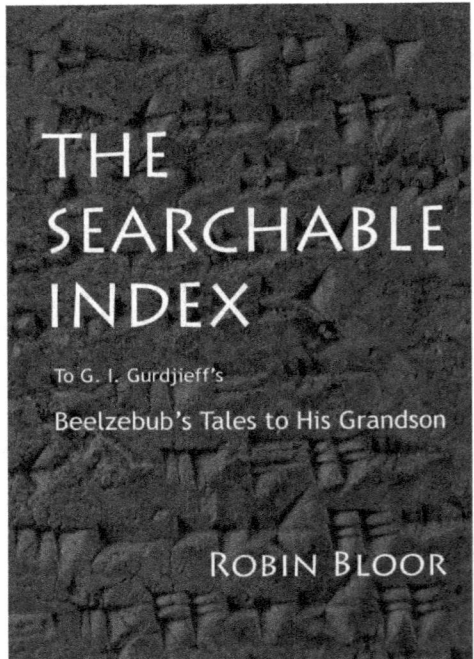

www.ingramcontent.com/pod-product-compliance
Lightning Source LLC
Chambersburg PA
CBHW020250030426

42336CB00010B/702